A Dog Owner's Guide to

Te...

Tetra○Press

16020

A Dog Owner's Guide to

Bull Terriers

Everything you need to know about your Bull Terrier,
including health care, breeding and showing

Dr. Dieter Fleig

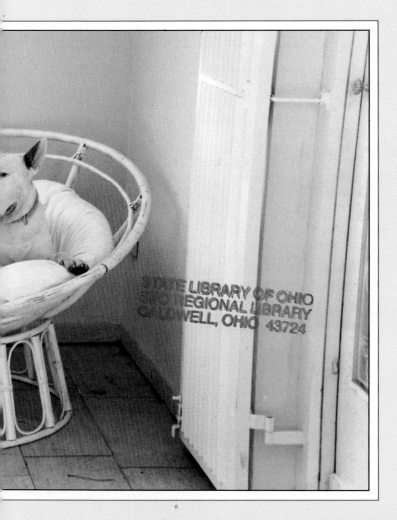

A Salamander Book

First published 1992 by KYNOS VERLAG Dr. Dieter Fleig GmbH,
Am Remelsbach 30, 54570 Mürlenbach/Eifel, Germany.
Copyright of the original German edition © 1992 KYNOS VERLAG
Dr. Dieter Fleig GmbH.

This English language edition © 1996 Salamander Books Ltd.
Published in North America by Tetra Press,
3001 Commerce Street,
Blacksburg, VA 24606

ISBN 1-56465-190-8

All correspondence concerning the content of this volume should be
addressed to Salamander Books Ltd., 129-137 York Way,
London N7 9LG, United Kingdom.

Contents

Typeset by SX Composing Ltd., Essex, United Kingdom.
Printed in China by Leefung Asco Printers Ltd.

Front cover photograph:
Ch. Double Dutch of Pitmans, Photographer: Markus Grossmann.

This oil painting of a Bull Terrier is by Renaud Ditte from a photograph by Jobrulu Jacobinia.

Preface

I wrote my first book about the Bull Terrier in 1970 at a time when this breed was not as widely known to dog-lovers in my home country of Germany as it is today. The title of this first book was *A Portrait of a Fascinating Breed*, and my initial fascination is still with me today and has since been adopted by numerous other dog owners. In 1970, 129 Bull Terrier puppies were born in Germany and this figure rose to 507 in 1980 and again to 1039 in 1989.

However, a dog breed has no greater enemy than a sharp increase in its popularity. Such an upsurge of interest attracts both the wrong sort of buyers and the wrong sort of breeders. It encourages breeders who become involved with the singular objective of making easy money and, in order to accommodate this change in membership, the clubs that were established to protect the best interests of the breed, make new arrangements and standards become more relaxed.

The Bull Terrier is possibly one of the most misunderstood and intensely abused breed of dog – a sad fact which has no doubt caused a great deal of damage to its reputation. Today, the Bull Terrier needs to be actively protected from such exploitation. With the kind permission of Ethologist, Dr. Dorit Feddersen-Petersen, I would like to quote the following from her contribution, *Why I Would Like A Bull Terrier To Be My Next Dog:*

"I have established a friendship with many Bull Terriers and I love their individuality and the way in which they so readily show affection for people – and the intensity of this. Furthermore, I like the robustness and endurance of this breed which comes to the fore during play and on long walks with their owners. I am particularly impressed by the 'imp-like' Bull Terrier behaviour and the ability these dogs have to adapt so well to their human companions that they almost develop similar characteristics. I consider myself to be a bit of an imp too, so the Bull Terrier is definitely the perfect dog for me!

Finally, I have a strong sense of justice and this drives me time and time again to identify with those who find themselves discriminated against and I would like to prove to the world what I already know – that Bull Terriers can be extremely lovable dogs if they are given proper care and allowed to develop in the way that they should. My Bull Terrier will most certainly be socially compatible with both people and other dogs!"

The original title of this book read: *Bull Terriers – How They Really Are, And Should Be*. It is my fourth book exclusively about this breed and you may well be wondering whether there is any new information left to impart.

Since 1958, I have kept at least one and often several Bull Terriers, totalling over 35 years of constant care and learning. In many of my previous books, I came to the subject as something of a breed enthusiast. However, I regard myself as an open-minded person who is capable of learning from past experiences and one who is keen to adapt to new practises. I am often shocked to see how thoughtless some of the people involved with this breed are and, having only their own best interests at heart, they act in an irresponsible manner, causing considerable damage to this breed and its reputation. I see this book as a means to redress these misconceptions and to encourage a fresh approach.

The basis of this book is formed by my true concern for this lovable breed. The Bull Terrier is a unique dog which possesses a character as individual and appealing as its offbeat appearance. I hope that this book will go some way toward encouraging responsible ownership of these dogs and to introduce all aspects of care to potential fanciers of this fascinating breed.

Dieter Fleig

The Bull Terrier's true character is lovable and family-orientated.
Photo: W. Bergerhausen

Chapter One

HISTORY OF THE BREED

An early Bull Terrier.   *Oil painting by Euphémie Muraton, 1880.*

All dog breeds have been created on the basis of man-made selections in order to achieve a dog that would serve a certain purpose and ideally embrace all the desirable features required to ensure excellent performance.

One has to remember though that, during the last century, this selection process focused primarily on work performance and that aesthetics were only of prime importance in a handful of breeds. However, the aforementioned work performances generally required a certain balance of anatomical features and character to deliver the best possible results.

Unfortunately, we tend to overlook the fact that almost all dog breeds were created to serve human purposes. In order to understand the character and anatomy of a dog, it is essential to identify its intended purpose. Sheep dogs, hounds, pointers, setters, greyhounds, sledge dogs – in all of these cases, the task put to the dogs formed the basis for character and anatomical requirements.

ABUSE OF THE DOG FOR ANIMAL FIGHTS

The Bull Terrier faced a difficult start to its development as it was bred with the intent purpose of being a fighting dog. In the name of sport, these dogs were pitted one against another in the pit – a fighting arena similar to the boxing ring. The breed was created in early Industrial England – a period in which the exploitation of the human workforce, child labour in mines and 16 hour working days for women in the home were generally accepted by society. This kind of exploitation extended, of course, to animals and came long before the Prevention of Cruelty to Animals act had ever been formulated.

'Panem et circenses' – 'Bread and games'! This concept was adopted by governments to keep the people happy and can be traced back to Ancient times to the arenas of the Romans where the suppressed masses were offered entertainment to make allowances for their sufferings. In the England of old, and indeed most countries of this time, brutal animal fights served as a valve which encouraged people to let off steam and so maintained subservience in the workforce.

Bulls, bears, lions, badgers and monkeys were all subjected to the relentless attacks of roused dogs, and the fight of dog against dog represented a particular attraction. If you would like to gain a better insight into the brutality of such animal fights, I recommend that you watch a bull fight in Spain or a cock fight in South America.

I do not mention these human aberrations because I approve of them – far from it – but because, in a way, they played an important role in the early development of the Bull Terrier breed. Its original role was that of Gladiator – to fight dog against dog.

JAMES HINKS – FATHER OF THE BULL TERRIER

James Hinks is generally regarded to be the founder of the breed and the initial breeds that he used were the English Bulldog (an experienced fighting dog) and the elegant White English Terrier. You will see from the images opposite, that these two breeds are considerably different where anatomy is concerned. On the one hand you have the heavy-weight, stocky Bulldog with a pronounced overshot jawline and, on the other, you have the slim, smart-looking

The English Bulldog.

Oil painting by J.T. Tuite, 1830.

White English Terrier.

Oil painting by E. Irsfeld, 1873.

Terrier. These variations constituted the root of many later breeding problems regarding a desirable standard bite and an anatomically uniform breed type. Today, we still differentiate between a Bulldog type and a Terrier type.

In addition, these breeds not only showed anatomical variations but also strong differences in character and temperament. James Hinks's objective was to combine the smart agility of the Terrier as a vermin hunter with the courage, endurance and stubbornness of the fighting Bulldog. This appeared to be the ideal combination in creating a dog which would make suitable sport in fighting other dogs. It has to be said, that he was not unsuccessful with regard to creating a uniform character. Unlike other terrier breeds, the Bull Terrier is difficult to irritate and has a great deal of affection for humans. However it also possesses the strength, wit and endurance of the Bulldog if provoked in a hostile manner.

James Hinks was successful in his aim to create a pit fighter that would also possess great affection for humans. His breeding, which was restricted to white dogs only, proved more than a match for the Staffordshire types. The triumphant march into the pit began for the early Bull Terrier toward the end of the 1800s. If you look at the painting shown on page 11, you will see an early example dating back to 1880 and it is astounding to note that, even at this stage, the bitch portrayed already displays standing ears.

DEVELOPMENT OF THE BREED AS A SHOW DOG

James Hinks presented his breed at dog shows right from the start.

This is why the Bull Terrier may be regarded as one of the dog breeds that competed alongside other dog breeds at the first English shows and were bred with a view to achieve a standard external appearance. One cannot deny that the pit represents this breed's starting point however, even in the early stages, breeders were making efforts to produce a breed which not only would deliver good performance but also a show dog with a beautiful appearance. Thus the Gladiator experienced its transformation into the White Knight! This represents a huge difference to the Staffordshire Terriers which found their way into the show ring as late as the 1930s.

Over the years, the objective of Bull Terrier breeding was to create a confident dog that could be harmoniously integrated into human daily life. Systematic breeding efforts reduced the dog's original desire to bare its teeth, however, every effort was made not to undermine the confidence associated with this breed.

COLOURED BULL TERRIERS

Problems occurred, temporarily, when it became necessary to find a natural way to achieve the standing ears due to new legislation passed in England which prevented the cropping of ears for this purpose. Quite a few heads were turned when breeders who preferred to take a long view crossed the white breed lines with Staffords to create a coloured Bull Terrier at the beginning of this century. Over the years, both of these breeding objectives were completed successfully and white and coloured varieties were crossed in such a manner that a standard, high level of quality was achieved and previous divisions no longer occurred.

Thanks to some extraordinary breeder personalities – at the top of the list, Raymond Oppenheimer, creator of the modern Bull Terrier and pictured below, the breed experienced anatomical development and achieved worldwide recognition in the relevant dog circles. The quality was so improved that, in 1972, the Bull Terrier Ch. Abraxas Audacity became the Crufts Supreme Champion. This recognition enabled the breed to move into the upper league of the international dog hierarchy.

Between 1960 and 1980, breeding of the English Bull Terrier reached its peak. In particular, the excellent kennel 'Romany' produced first class coloured Bull Terriers and, due to Miss Montague Johnstone, coloured Bull Terriers and white Bull Terriers were finally regarded of equal quality. The photograph on page 16 shows the three great breeders of the white variety – Raymond Oppenheimer (Ormandy), Eva Weatherill (Souperlative) and Margaret O. Sweeten (Agate's).

Raymond Oppenheimer – Creator of the modern Bull Terrier.
Photo: Dr. Fleig.

BULL TERRIERS AROUND THE WORLD

The history of this breed, of course, extends to the breeding efforts in numerous other countries. In 1887, 20 Bull Terriers were presented in a show ring in Stuttgart, Germany. However, annual breed figures remained rather on the low side and for many years there were no registrations at all; some referred to this as 'occasional' breeding.

Even in the 1960s, annual registrations were far below 100 puppies. The 1970s and 1980s represented the break-through for this breed and, today, the Bull Terrier enjoys much popularity in Germany. In 1989, it took the 16th place among a total of 176 breeds registered with the Verband für das Deutsche Hundewesen e.V. (VDH).

In Austria, Holland and Switzerland, the popularity of the Bull Terrier has been on the

Raymond Oppenheimer, Eva Weatherill, Margaret O. Sweeten – three of the great British breeders. *Photo: Dr. Fleig.*

increase and some breeders in these countries have a considerable influence on continental breeding. The United States of America and Canada are considered today to be on an equal par with the United Kingdom where the Bull Terrier breed is concerned. In the United States, this breed was already historically documented in 1869. In South Africa this breed thrives particularly well, and its rate of 3,000 puppies, annually beats all other countries!

During its 130 year breed history, the Bull Terrier has secured a leading position and is now considered to be among the top twenty breeds. It offers a wealth of pleasure to its friends and you will find all the important aspects relating to this dog breed highlighted here in this guide.

The young Bull Terrier.   *Photo: G. Michel.*

Chapter Two

BREED STANDARD

This drawing shows a male dog with a very typical Bull Terrier head. The head is well-filled and has an expression typical of this breed. The only noticeable fault in this example is that the flews are too full.

WHAT IS A BREED STANDARD?

Please do not skip this chapter! I know that Standard phrases do not always make for easy reading and you may feel that such a detailed analysis is not of any relevance to you if you intend your Bull Terrier to be just a family pet. However, I still believe that it is essential to read and understand these as they will give you a clearer understanding of the ideal for your dog's anatomy and may give early clues to physical irregularities which may lead to health problems later.

A Breed Standard is a set of descriptions relating to the specific dog breed which is set by the county of origin; it lists all the requirements that a top breed dog must fulfil in order to be successful at shows and to win top titles. Every aspect of the dog's physical features and temperament which combine to make a breed such as its anatomy, character, weight, coat, gait and movement, is stipulated in the Standard. A good Standard may be recognised by the fact that you will find the performance of a dog at the top of the list, followed by health, and that the desired temperament is described in detail.

Even if you have no intention of presenting your dog at a show, I would still strongly recommend that you read this chapter to familiarise yourself with the ideals of this breed, even if you have exclusively acquired your dog to be a common household pet. For a good Standard describes the ideal dog and your family pet should resemble this as closely as possible. I admit that, even among we humans, not all of us are physical beauties but, nevertheless, each of us has our strong points. However, good physical and mental health are desirable ingredients for any life be it human or canine.

Reading through the Standard, you may find that some of the descriptions seem exaggerated and may even encourage excesses in breeding in some cases. This matter is investigated in the sub-chapter 'Explanation of Standard Phrases' which follows the descriptions of the Standard and may further explain any matters which remain unclear.

Please read the whole chapter and study the drawings produced by Cynthia Lord-Ruddy which, in my opinion, are particularly successful in illustrating the anatomical pointers of the Standard. You should find that once you have completed this chapter, you will have gained an invaluable insight into this breed and will have come to understand what truly makes a good Bull Terrier.

England is the land of origin of the Bull Terrier and, according to international breeding regulations, the Standard sovereignty remains with the mother country. In the case of the Bull Terrier, the final breeding Standard for the breed is stipulated by the Kennel Club of Great Britain. The Standard, as described by the country of origin, is binding.

English Standard of the Bull Terrier
Revised 01.07.1986

GENERAL APPEARANCE –
Strongly built, muscular, well-balanced and active with a keen, determined and intelligent expression.

CHARACTERISTICS –
The Bull terrier is the Gladiator of the canine race, full of fire and courage. A unique feature is a down-faced, egg-shaped head.

Pictured above is a male Bull Terrier with excellent body proportions. It has a beautiful, well-filled head and no sign of the disproportionate 'Down-face'. It has very good ears, excellent eyes and a beautiful neck and first class backline. The well-muscled body shows a suitably closed front and there is excellent angulation, good bones and feet.

Irrespective of size, dogs should look masculine and bitches feminine.

TEMPERAMENT –
Of even temperament and amenable to discipline. Although obstinate, is particularly good with people.

HEAD AND SKULL –
Head long, strong and deep right to end of muzzle, but not coarse. Viewed from front, egg-shaped and completely filled, its surface free from hollows or indentations. Top of skull almost flat from ear to ear. Profile curves gently downward from top of skull to tip of nose which should be black and bent downward at the tip. Nostrils well developed and underjaw deep and strong.

MOUTH –
Teeth sound, clean, strong, of good size, regular with a perfect regular and complete scissor bite, i.e. upper teeth closely overlapping lower teeth and set square to the jaws. Lips clean and tight.

EYES –
Appearing narrow, obliquely placed and triangular, well sunken, black or as dark brown as possible so as to appear almost black, and with a piercing glint. Distance from tip of nose to eyes perceptively greater than that from eyes to top of skull. Blue or partly blue undesirable.

EARS –
Small, thin and placed close together. Dog should be able to

This is how a good Bull Terrier should look. Note the strong, broad chest, straight bones and beautiful, closed feet. The eye shape is first class, with the area below well-filled. The ear position is also good.

This example shows common faults. Note the badly-formed front with bow legs, faulty head with broad ear line, soft ears and a forehead furrow, the hollowed area under the eyes and the short atypical neck.

hold them stiffly erect, when they point straight upwards.

NECK – Very muscular, long, arched, tapering from shoulders to head and free from loose skin.

FOREQUARTERS –
Shoulders strong and muscular without loading. Shoulder blades wide, flat and held close to the chest wall and have a very pronounced backward slope of front edge from bottom to top, forming almost a right angle with upper arm. Elbows held straight and strong, pasterns upright. Forelegs have strongest type of round, quality bone, dog should stand solidly upon them and they should be perfectly parallel. In mature dogs, length of foreleg should be approximately equal to depth of chest.

BODY –
Body well rounded with marked spring of ribs and great depth from withers to brisket, so that latter nearer the ground than the belly. Back short, strong with backline behind withers level, arching or roaching slightly over broad, well-muscled loins. Underline from brisket to belly forms a graceful upward curve. Chest broad when viewed from front.

HINDQUARTERS –
Hindlegs in parallel when viewed from behind. Thighs muscular and second thighs well developed. Stifle joint well bent and hock well angulated with bone to foot short and strong.

FEET –
Round and compact with well-arched toes.

TAIL –
Short, set on low and carried horizontally. Thick at root, it tapers to a fine point.

GAIT/MOVEMENT –
When moving appears well knit, smoothly covering ground with free, easy strides and with a typical jaunty air. When trotting, movement parallel, front and back; only converging towards centre line at faster speeds, forelegs reaching out well and hindlegs moving smoothly at hip, flexing well at stifle and hock, with great thrust.

COAT –
Short, flat even and harsh to touch with a fine gloss. Skin fitting dog tightly. A soft textured undercoat may be present in winter.

COLOUR –
For white, pure white coat. Skin pigmentation and markings on head not to be penalised. For coloured, colour predominates; all other things being equal, brindle preferred. Black brindle, red, fawn and tri-colour acceptable. Tick markings in white coat undesirable. Blue and liver highly undesirable.

SIZE –
There are neither height nor weight limits, but there should be the impression of maximum substance for the size of dog, consistent with quality and sex.

FAULTS –
Any departure from the foregoing points should be considered a fault and the seriousness with which the fault should be regarded should be in exact proportion to its degree.

NOTE – Male Bull Terriers should have two apparently normal testicles which are fully descended into the scrotum. Abnormalities here are considered a fault.

EXPLANATION OF THE STANDARD PHRASES

First of all, I would like to say that I think that the Breed Standard of the Bull Terrier is a clear and accurate one. Compared with the initial Standard phrases which were stipulated in the last century, today's text has seen very few changes. This indicates that the early breeders took a long term view of the anatomy and character of the dog which also ensured the continuation of the breed. Problems concerning the interpretation of individual phrases have only arisen due to some incidences of wilfully wrong approaches by show judges or national breed organisations. Below I have given wider explanations of each of the clauses in the Standard which I hope will clarify the meaning of any indistinct statements and give you a greater understanding of the requirements set out by the Breed Standard.

General appearance –
Its strong well-muscled body must always be aligned with the gait or movement of the dog, giving it a natural ease of movement. A dog's expression reflects its temperament and, in the case of the Bull Terrier, this should be lively, confident and intelligent.

Characteristics –
The title 'Gladiator' should be replaced with 'White Knight' and this type of reference should only be considered valid when referring to the historical background of the breed. The egg-shaped skull with its down-face differentiates this breed very clearly from any other. Unfortunately, the relevant Standard phrases have encouraged breeding excesses regarding the desired head form.

Temperament –
Despite misguided beliefs that Bull Terriers are aggressive and may constitute a threat to humans, the Breed Standard quite rightly underlines their affection for humans and their happiness to accept their place in the human hierarchy. Breeders who continue to promote a distinctive fighting lust should turn their attentions to other dog breeds as, in doing so, they are creating Bull Terriers which fail to fulfil the breed requirements.

Head and skull –
Unfortunately, as is the case with all dog breeds, there is often too much emphasis placed on the creation of an ideal head form. Judges should remember that the head is only one part of the dog's anatomy and its appearance should not be overrated – 'A dog does not run on its head' (Tom Horner). The Standard describes the desired head form in an easy to understand manner, however, this does not necessarily mean that the Bull Terrier should be judged on its head shape alone – a healthy anatomical structure is just as important!

Mouth –
The Standard requirements suggest that a scissor bite is ideal and both overshot and undershot jaws are considered faulty. Particular attention should be paid not only to the position of the incisors but also the canines and the molars when examining the bite. Distortion of the bite to an overshot or undershot bite does not affect the incisors but will affect the position of the molar teeth and the function of these may be affected by distorted gearing teeth. A too narrow lower jaw is considered a serious fault as, in such a case, the lower

fangs will damage the upper jaw. The undershot jaw should also not be played down as this causes the lower incisors to damage the upper palate and an affected dog will find it difficult and uncomfortable to eat. In England, the term 'complete' relates only to the full set of incisors and not to the number of premolar and molar teeth.

These days you may often come across Bull Terriers with overly heavy flews (sides of lips) which is neither attractive nor desirable. In the case of the Bull Terrier, you will also often come across dogs with an overshot bite, a hereditary Bulldog quality. However it is worth mentioning that, when considering the seriousness of a fault, a medium overshot affects a dog's health and well-being less than an undershot. One should remember that, in the case of numerous other breeds, the Standard expressly demands an overshot jaw.

Eyes –
The oblique position of the eyes is very typical for this breed and so is their triangular shape. Round, goggle eyes are not desirable in this breed. Dark eyes with a characteristic piercing glint are again very typical for this breed and much desired.

Ears –
Heavy dogs often have more of a problem with the position of the ears than their lightweight counterparts. Obliquely placed ears are not considered attractive. A correct ear position in accordance with the Standard phrase is a typical feature of this breed.

Neck –
Unfortunately, the word 'long' is very often overlooked and we are left with too many bull-necks or short necks. The neck form as described in the Standard is an essential part of the correct Bull Terrier anatomy.

Forequarters –
The Standard description is excellent and its meaning quite clear. However, in practical terms, correct shoulder formation – the typical Bull Terrier front – with closely set elbows, is often not achieved. Also, many of today's Bull Terriers lack sufficient length in their leg bones. The desired ratio of length of forelegs matching the depth of chest remains unaccomplished in the case of many dogs and short-leggedness continues to prevail. Please study the anatomy drawings of this chapter!

Body –
In this case too, the Standard description is perfect. However, far too many Bull Terrier fanciers cannot distinguish between substance and obesity. This leads to many dogs carrying too much extra weight and we see soft backs and pendulous abdomens. It seems that the presence of an elegant lower line has become something of a rarity.

Hindquarters –
More attention should be paid to the correct angulation of the knee and the ankle joint as requested by the Standard. Bow-leggedness is a common problem among many of today's dogs.

Feet –
Most of today's Bull Terriers fulfil the Standard requirements in this area. So-called 'hare's feet' do not comply with the Standard.

Tail –
In the case of the Terrier type, we

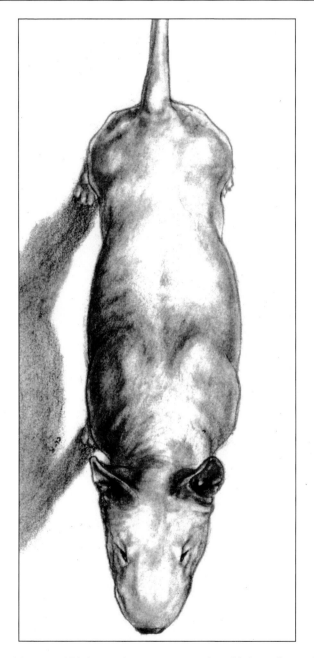

From this unusual birds-eye view, you can see the athletic, well-muscled body structure, the pronounced spring of ribs and the waist formation in the loin area. The desirable substance required by the Standard is achieved by a well-muscled body without any flabbiness or paunch caused by obesity.

will frequently find that the tail is set too high and often runs parallel to too-steeply angulated hindquarters. The 'gay tail' – the happily lifted tail – is not a sign of a particularly cheerful character but is an anatomical fault. The Standard stipulates that the tail be horizontal.

Movement/gait –
Compared with other dog breeds, the Bull Terrier faces more than its fair share of difficulties when it comes to graceful movement – compact dogs simply cannot move with the easy elegance of their lightweight counterparts. Bearing this in mind, it is all the

more important to pay special attention to a dog of this breed's movement. The Standard description has been revised to make it absolutely clear and there should be no mistaking the importance of achieving good results in this area. The illustrations here certainly help to provide a better understanding of how good anatomy can produce a better gait. These days, we can enjoy a far higher number of graceful Bull Terriers which exhibit excellent movement.

Unfortunately, efforts to achieve this improvement have also been responsible for creating a longer than desired back. There is still a

This front view shows how the front remains well-closed during movement. When trotting, the legs have a parallel motion.

long way to go until we see dogs which truly conform with the Standard in this area.

Coat and colour –

There are very few problems surrounding the coat and colour as the Standard phrases express a very clear view of this matter. One should remember that although faulty markings may immediately catch everybody's eye, they do not affect the dog's abilities in any way. An outward turned elbow or too steeply angulated hindquarters will affect the physical stature and movement of a dog in a way that a simple discolouration of the coat can not. A faulty colour constitutes a typical 'beauty spot' which may hinder your dog's ability to achieve top show titles, but this should not affect your dog in any other way.

Size and weight –

The Standard description is almost ideal and this breed has remained in the medium size range for over a hundred years despite the lack of accuracy in describing shoulder size or weight limits.

Exaggerations tend to produce oversized and heavy-weight dogs which affect the dogs' mobility. It is important to bear in mind that maximum substance refers to bone and muscle mass and is

Faulty movement is often seen and, in this case, the paws paddle.

certainly no excuse for obesity or an overly-large paunch – sadly, conditions which one encounters time and time again. A paunch contradicts the Standard with regards to the under-line and is

Wise judges and breeders know that the Standard is all about looking at the good points of a dog and this positive view should not be overshadowed. It would be wrong to judge dogs (and indeed

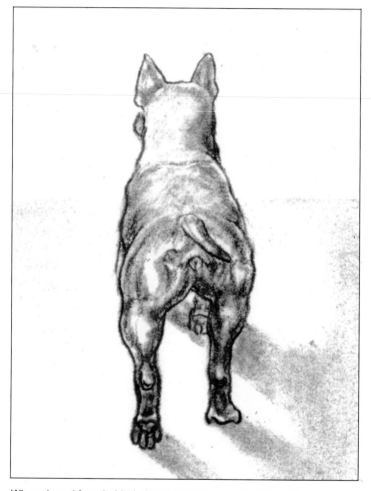

When viewed from behind, there should be excellent thrust from the hindquarters and the legs should run parallel.

not conducive to good health.

Faults –
With all this talk of faults, it would be easy to lose sight of what is important when judging a dog.

people) primarily by their faults.

THE MINIATURE BULL TERRIER

From the early beginnings of the pure breeding efforts in the

1860s, separate categories for the Miniature Bull Terrier were established at shows. It is the size and weight categories that separate the Miniature Bull Terrier from the standard variety. These

early as 1906. In 1918, the Kennel Club closed further registrations as no applications had been made.

In 1939, Colonel Glyn founded a separate club for the Miniature

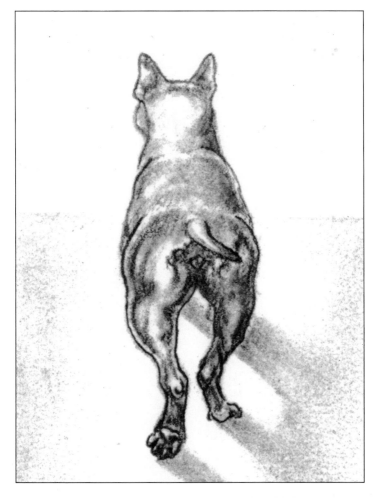

In a bad example, note the bow-legged position of the hindquarters which produces insufficient thrust.

lightweight dogs became particularly popular with English fanciers over one hundred years ago. However, due to the imposed size or weight limits, the breed nearly faced extinction as

Bull Terrier and encouraged a new interest in the breed.

The fundamental problem in breeding the Miniature Bull Terrier is that, genetically, all miniature forms of dog breeds tend to

The illustrations above show how a dog should move in accordance with the Standard. When moving, the dog has a well-knit appearance and covers the ground with free, easy steps. The forelegs reach out well and the hindlegs move smoothly from the hip.

produce dogs with the commonly seen apple-shape eyes (round eyes) associated with miniature breeding. However, it is stipulated that a Miniature Bull Terrier is supposed to retain a typical Bull Terrier head and this includes its distinctive oblique, triangular eyes. The second, almost unsolvable problem was that, until a few years ago, a strict weight limit existed. So, how was one supposed to fulfil the requirements of the Standard with regard to maximum substance?

Today the Miniature Bull Terrier should resemble the standard Bull Terrier in every way other than stature – it may only possess a maximum shoulder height of 14 inches (35cm) and all weight limits have been abandoned. Still the task of breeding the Miniature Bull Terrier has not become significantly easier.

In England, the country of origin of this breed, one was allowed to cross old miniature breeds with Bull Terriers that had successfully maintained a small size over quite a number of years. However, a Bull Terrier of small appearance, a phenotype, still carries the gene for the size of the standard Bull Terrier. So, it comes as no surprise that exact predictions as to how many whelps of a Miniature Bull Terrier litter will in fact fulfil the set size limits are extremely difficult.

There are quite a number of Bull Terrier owners who, due to the limited size of their home,

would quite happily have chosen a Miniature Bull Terrier. The ever-growing demand for the smaller Staffordshire Bull Terrier also goes some way to validate the demand for smaller dogs of this type.

As mentioned earlier, the Miniature Bull Terrier is an exact copy of the standard Bull Terrier complete with its charming Bull Terrier temperament, therefore the breeding of good Miniature Bull Terriers certainly makes for a wonderful and worthwhile challenge.

Breeders have long underestimated or failed to recognise the potential of these little fellows and have hesitated, not without reason, to tackle this difficult breeding task. The Miniature Bull Terrier is a most interesting dog breed with a great potential for development once these initial breeding problems have been overcome.

In this context, I would like to recall a discussion I had with my friend Raymond Oppenheimer during which we spoke about these very breeding problems. He expressed his opinion by asking the following question: 'Do you think that if I had commenced with the breeding of the Miniature Bull Terrier in the 1930s that today's breed would be successfully crossed and the breeding problems solved?' My reply simply had to be 'yes' – after all, success in these areas is almost certainly always a matter of a breeder's determination to succeed.

In accordance with the Terrier type, this example shows an excellent, correctly filled head, beautiful small ears, an elegant neck and short

back. The tail is beautifully set in a continuous line from the spine. There
is good bone structure, correct leg length and good angulation.

In the Bulldog type, there is a strongly-pronounced upper head, disproportionate flews, strong lower jaw and strong neck. The deep chest

has a well-developed forechest, the feet are too broad and the leg bones too short compared with the depth of the chest.

Chapter Three

SELECTION AND PURCHASE

Bingo is a fine 12 week old male from the Abraxas kennel.

WHO IS THE IDEAL OWNER OF A BULL TERRIER?

I believe that if Bull Terriers had the opportunity to choose their owners, rather than the other way round, there would be far fewer problems resulting from unsuitable placements. For dogs have very good instincts which tell them whether they are looking at good company or not, whilst we humans approach this matter rather differently and often with misguided preconceptions. We cultivate high expectations and ideals with regard to our future four-legged friend and are often ill-prepared for the responsibility which comes with this new arrival.

In this respect, Bull Terrier purchasers are no different from other would-be dog owners although fortunately, I have to admit, it appears that most Bull Terrier friends have a good idea about the nature of the dog they intend to purchase and bring along some previous knowledge of the breed. However this in itself can be a problem as, in this case, they go to the breeder with their heads filled with preconceptions and illusions! For the majority of people seeking to buy a Bull Terrier, this breed is simply their 'dream dog'. Well, to be perfectly honest, I was under just the same illusion when I went to buy my first Bull Terrier.

The fighting spirit

The Gladiator among dog breeds, the White Knight . . . the fact that the ownership of such a 'wonder dog' poses some clear demands on the owner is one that we are only confronted with at a much later date!

The Bull Terrier is not suitable for authoritarian dog fanciers. However, it is not an entirely suitable choice for the soft-hearted either as this dog doesn't hesitate in taking advantage of weak, inconsequential training. To quote an English expert, it is: 'A dog that does not tolerate an idiot as its owner.'

It is not without reason that I have included details of this breed's historical background and its fight for survival in the pit in this book. Such a dog requires determination, independence, courage and perseverance – all qualities that exclude any form of blind obedience, yet the Breed Standard emphasises its benevolence and affection for humans. This is a true, hereditary fighting dog quality which is very often misunderstood by the uninitiated. In the pit, dogs which were fighting each other to the death would be separated by men during the breaks and, during the fight, the dog owners were able to kneel close to their battling Gladiators. The ready acceptance of human company is a salient trait of the Bull Terrier – just imagine trying to separate German Shepherds or Terriers with your bare hands during a fight! Its very nature encourages the Bull Terrier to approach a stranger with confidence and bearing no aggression but, if things get tough, this dog knows how to defend itself. However, you will find that a correctly-trained Bull Terrier will not demonstrate any aggressive behaviour toward people and I whole-heartedly object to the training of Bull Terriers as guard dogs, as is often seen today.

A sweet-natured companion

If you are interested in this breed, may I ask you to not just look at the small Gladiator but at the affection-seeking, cuddly dog as well. I am aware of very few other breeds that are so much in need of their daily cuddles and this appears to be an inherently typical Bulldog quality. Time and time again, we have discussed how to put into practise a suitable 'cuddling system' for our own Bull Terriers – that great is their need for affection. Cosiness is the other thing they simply adore and the human bed is hardly ever spared a visit. Snuggling in the bed is just delightful to them and even more wonderful than snuggling on the soft cushioned armchairs.

In addition to their affectionate nature, Bull Terriers are also lovable clowns and it is not difficult for our human imaginations to attribute a sense of humour to them! Bull Terriers are dogs for happy people who enjoy a hearty joke and are able to smile from ear to ear about themselves and their dogs.

Providing for the dog's needs
And so now let us return to the demands that a Bull Terrier makes on its owner. First and foremost, you must be able to provide plenty of time to spend with your dog as this breed needs human company to feel wholly comfortable. This is not a dog that is suitable for those who work full-time and have no choice but to leave their dog alone for eight to ten hours a day. All the more, it is an ideal children's dog as it needs little encouragement to play. In fact, it is a dog for the whole family!

I have already mentioned the Bull Terrier's strong individuality, and some people refer to this as obstinacy. Because of this quality, a Bull Terrier requires a master or mistress who is able to provide firm, logical but affectionate training. This does not constitute harsh treatment, physical punishment or even a tormenting training collar, but it is advisable that a young Bull Terrier learns its position within the family hierarchy and the boundaries of acceptable behaviour right from the start. Proper training is a condition for living together in harmony – and, of course, lots of affection.

With regard to offering a suitable home in the physical sense, the Bull Terrier is a rather modest dog which does not require a great deal of space. It is a suitable dog to keep in an apartment as it is happy to sleep a lot of the time provided it receives enough exercise and plenty of attention from its two-legged owner. Its daily exercise requirements are also modest compared to other breeds with half hour sessions in the morning, at lunchtime and again in the evening constituting the minimum. At weekends, your dog will appreciate a long walk in the woods or park and, if you do not have access to wide open spaces, a long session of active play in a local park should provide sufficient exercise to keep your Bull Terrier fit and healthy.

Counting the costs
There are many benefits to be gained by owning a Bull Terrier but, before purchase, you must give careful consideration to your ability to fulfil your new responsibilities and to the other factors involved such as financial costs. In weighing up these factors, you need to account for feeding costs, taxes, indemnity insurance, the cost of vaccinations and veterinary bills and, last but not least, the purchase price of the puppy itself, which will be by no means cheap.

You will find more information about living with your pet in the chapters referring to the young and adult Bull Terrier.

The Bull Terrier's sweet nature and willingness to play makes it an ideal dog for a family with children. Photo: Manuela Barth.

THE PURCHASE OF A BULL TERRIER PUPPY

When purchasing a puppy, there are two main factors that you will need to look into in some depth and these are the puppy's parents and the breeder. Both of these areas are of equal importance. You can gain a good idea of the future form of a puppy by looking at its ancestors. The genes of the male dog and bitch will determine the quality of the puppy with regard to the set Breed Standards (you should refer to Chapter Six for more details).

In this chapter, let me just go as far as to recommend that you have a good look at the bitch and,

if possible, the male dog too. Only if both animals meet your personal expectations of a good Bull Terrier to an acceptable degree should you consider purchasing a pup from this mating. Even more illuminating, would be the chance to meet young Bull Terriers of a previous litter. Grandparents, parents, uncles, aunts and siblings can all give you clues to the form of the puppies, so see them all if you can as this will give you all the more confidence in how the selected pup will develop at a later stage. Remember – all puppies are sweet and tempting, it is what they will be like later and how they will develop that should be your priority.

Choosing a suitable breeder

The difference in quality between breeders can vary enormously and this is often the case with popular breeds which carry high purchase prices and can attract the wrong kind of breeders only too easily. Some disreputable individuals only have their own financial interests at heart and lack the dedication required to rear successful puppies.

Responsible breeders hardly ever hit the good time. Good breeding practice costs money and demands even more spare time! Studies of dog behaviour have established that it is during the rearing phase – whilst the dog is still with the breeder – that the dog's character for life is determined, for better or for worse. Correct feeding of the bitch and good kennel conditions may be important, but human care is just as vital. Whelps need plenty of human contact along with the chance to play and ample opportunity to become familiar with their exciting environment if they are to mature into good dogs.

Kennel conditions

Ideally, puppies should not grow up in a sterile kennel without contact with other dogs and humans, but should always spend their first three weeks in a human home environment where the breeder can monitor both puppies and mothers thoroughly. Thereafter, they may be accommodated in their own breed room which should allow them access to a designated area outside at a later date. Again, this room should not isolate the puppies, but encourage plenty of contact with humans.

A litter of puppies at three weeks of age.   *Photo: Ritschel.*

All puppies are sweet and tempting. When choosing an individual, your priority is to gauge what it will be like later and how it will develop as an adult dog.   *Photo: Gabriele Niestroj.*

There are breeders who do not allow visitors close contact with the puppies citing reasons of hygiene. In these cases, either the breeder has something to hide or their breeding methods are just plain outdated. However, visitors who have been in contact with sick dogs should, of course, not enter the kennel. Still the theoretical threat of possibly transmitting a disease from a visitor to the pups is the lesser of evils considering the vital contact with humans that the puppies need during this phase. For this is the phase during which the foundation is laid for its so-attractive naivety and its open-minded attitude toward us. Bull Terriers which experience isolation during this phase will demonstrate bad behaviour patterns as adults. It is, of course, the breeder's obligation to see that his or her puppies have only positive experiences with humans; puppies are most certainly not toys for children!

At approximately five weeks of age, the pups should be given the opportunity to gain new experiences in an appropriate exercising ground. Experts are calling for an adventure kennel which does not just primarily suit the breeder in that it easy to clean, but creates a stimulating environment which offers plenty of learning experiences for the puppy. Rough wood pieces, hard rubber balls, up-turned boxes to hide in, knotted ropes for towing games – all of these accessories offer the rowdy little pups the chance to develop their play with their littermates.

A final note with regard to selecting the right breeder. In my opinion he or she is responsible for bringing the puppies into the world and this responsibility should not end once the cheque has been cleared, but should apply throughout the whole of a dog's life! So, if your breeder asks you critical, even unpleasant, questions in order to gain a better idea about the environment his puppy is going to live in and, if not satisfied with your answers, even refuses to sell the puppy to you, then this is just the sort of breeder you should be looking for.

The future Bull Terrier owner should feel assured that he or she may go back to the breeder at any time to seek advice should any difficulties arise with the new family member. Some breeders prefer to establish a contract which gives them the right to buy the puppy back should it require placement with someone else and this is quite acceptable. I just wish that breeders would also feel obliged to take their puppies back should the health of the puppy require this.

Choosing a puppy

Just a few words with regard to the selection of a puppy. Even at an early stage, the pup's conformity with the Standard will be apparent and this applies in particular to the shape of its body – strong bones, well-ribbed up chest, correct angulation of forequarters and hindquarters. Substance is vital and so do not feel tempted to choose formless 'paunch pigs'; correctly reared pups will demonstrate good mobility and have a detectable waist and normal body form.

Evaluation of the head form is slightly more difficult. Let me draw on experience: A very typical head with well-rounded upper line and the correct fullness below the eyes rarely deteriorates later, however, this is frequently associated with overshot jaws. In the case of other head forms, there is a chance that they may well develop for the better, but this cannot be guaranteed.

Incorrect jaw alignment

In some pups, the overshot jaw may correct itself and develop into a normal scissor bite, however, in ninety percent of all cases this fault remains for life. Many breeders play down the undershot jaw and even praise it as a sure sign for the development of a scissor bite. Be careful because, although this does apply to some breed lines, it is not true of each and every case. The undershot jaw constitutes a serious handicap for the young pup and makes normal feeding quite difficult. Examine the upper jaw as an undershot jaw causes the low incisors to cut into it, causing pain. According to my own experience, I have to say that wrongly positioned lower jaws do not change but develop to a so-called wry mouth which represents a serious fault. Still more problematic is the occurrence of a too narrow lower jaw – a hereditary quality in the Terrier. In such a case, the lower canines do not appear in front of the upper teeth but far back behind in the upper jaw. The afflicted dog bites holes into its own upper jaw which is painful and very often requires the removal of the crowns of the teeth. This is a serious anatomical fault and the dog should be excluded from breeding!

Other faults

Less of a problem is a not yet fully coloured nose bridge appearing at the age of approximately eight weeks; this will usually develop satisfactorily in ninety percent of all cases. However, be careful if the parents of the pup also show signs of weak pigmentation.

A slight umbilical rupture is acceptable as this will not require an operation in most cases. Don't let your veterinarian talk you into an operation unless the umbilical rupture is at least the size of a walnut.

If you choose a male puppy carefully examine its testicles. Ensure that both testicles have moved down into the scrotum and, if necessary, have your veterinarian examine this. In most countries, deviation from the Standard in this area is commonly regarded as a serious fault and the dog will be excluded from breeding.

It is generally recommended that you should agree that the pup be examined by a veterinarian at the expense of the buyer before any purchase agreement becomes valid. Trust may be good, but a thorough examination is better!

Colouration

Undesirable white or coloured spots on certain parts of the body do not have any significance for a family pet's life and some people even love these spots. However, it is not regarded as particularly beautiful if a closed tabby or red back coat is asymmetrically split by a larger white spot. In the case of white dogs, coloured spots – with the exception of the head – are undesirable, but these do not bother the dog for a minute. One should remember the old equestrian saying: 'A good horse has no bad colours!' This also applies to the less popular Bull Terrier colour varieties such as black and the tri-colour.

Temperament

An examination of the pup's character is as important as an examination regarding anatomical preferences and faults. In the case of each dog family, you will come across a hierarchy and this is detectable even in a young litter of five to six weeks old. In their early days, the pups have a great propensity to learn and a pup knows quite soon which of its brothers and sisters should be avoided and which are the ones that give orders that are worth following. Do not get the strange idea that the head of the pack is the ideal dog for you! At a later stage it will try to get its own way and will demand considerable training by its master or mistress. Such a dog may be suitable for an experienced dog owner, but certainly not for the novice!

The puppy at the bottom of the pack hierarchy is also only a dog for fanciers. Quite frankly, given

From puppy to adulthood, Bull Terriers are cuddly dogs.

Photo: Moschner.

The young puppies' curiosity is boundless.　　　　　*Photo: Michel.*

the robust character of this breed, the 'wall flower' of the pack constitutes almost no problem – some people even fall in love with such a 'sensitive' creature. Many such puppies have shown excellent development later in life, however, caution should be exercised. Look at the characters of its parents and other close relatives. If you find any signs of shyness or anxiety then do not choose this 'wall flower' and I personally would not buy any pup from such a litter. Confidence is a typical character of the Bull Terrier and should not be compromised. Unfortunately, this is exactly what a large number of breeders have practised for the last twenty to thirty years to ensure show success!

Let's return to our litter. The right pup for the fancier is very often neither the most impudent nor the most sensitive, but simply the one in the middle! If both parents have a solid character, one might quite rightly expect that their pups will grow up to be ideal family pets and are cut out for a harmonious human-dog relationship. This tends to be true provided that proper training is ensured.

Evaluating the puppies in the kennel

So, how do you determine the place of an individual puppy in the pack? An interested buyer visits a litter of four and eight week old pups several times, sits down for half an hour and watches them. If you can spare this time and are successful in convincing the breeder that all you want to do is watch and not engage the pups in any kind of experiment, then you will soon see how the individual pup behaves when playing with its mother or brothers and sisters. This 'watch' is quite enjoyable, too!

There are puppy tests which have been establisheed by ethologists, however, their correct execution requires a great deal of sensitivity and 'dog-mindedness'. Generally a good breeder who maintains daily contact with his puppies should be able to recommend the dog with the character that will best suit you, after all, who else would know the pups better?

This, of course depends on the reliability of the breeder. In this context I would like to give this advice: If the breeder acts strangely in whatever way and a solid basis of trust cannot be established, it is best to go elsewhere.

Choosing the right puppy demands a few basic require-ments from its future owner:
1. Knowledge of the Breed Standard (it is worth reading Chapter Two again thoroughly so that you may be able to recall the most important facts). Only when comparing the parents with this Standard will you be able to evaluate the pups that you are watching play.
2. You also need to be familiar with the basics of dog behaviour as this constitutes the key to enabling you to evaluate the pup's character and temperament correctly. Always remember that the conditions and environment provided by the breeder of your choice will have an enormous influence on the puppy and this influence will remain with it for the rest of its life. Avoid single kennels at all costs if puppies appear neglected, dirty or psychologically depressed. Never buy a puppy just to put it out of its misery! This will no doubt result in you paying the purchase price over and over again for medical treatment of psychological defects which rarely ever disappear completely. It is not

The adventure kennel provides plenty of new learning opportunities.

At this tender age, everything is exciting and new.   *Photos: G. Michel.*

without reason that the puppy phase is described as the phase of the dog's life that forms its character! Think of it as a new coin – it gets stamped only once. If you insist on purchasing such a puppy out of the goodness of your heart, you are effectively endorsing poor breeding conditions and are encouraging less-respectable breeders to continue with their unsatisfactory trade!

Should you come across really dreadful breeding conditions, do not hesitate to take action for the sake of the dogs. Such establishments should be reported to the breed club and to the RSPCA. By making a stand and sticking to your guns, you will save helpless animals a great deal of misery!

THE PURCHASE OF AN ADULT BULL TERRIER

Those of you who have read my recommendations regarding the purchase of a puppy will most certainly have noted a number of basic considerations which also apply to the purchase of an adolescent or adult Bull Terrier. The scope of the above sub-chapter reflects the fact that, fortunately, most dogs are purchased at an age of between seven and eight weeks directly from a breeder.

Contrary to general opinion, the purchase of a Bull Terrier above said age group constitutes a higher risk than the purchase of a puppy. Although I admit that, for breeders looking for dogs which conform to a number of anatomical criteria, the purchase of a six month old or even fully-grown Bull Terrier may be of interest as risks regarding the development of anatomical defects are reduced. At this age, you can be sure that the dog has a complete set of teeth (although the significance of this requirement is

disputed) and this can only be established after the puppy's milk teeth have been shed. On several occasions, I have been forced to import older Bull Terriers, mainly due to intricate, narrow-minded, breeding regulations. But, for the fancier who is primarily looking for a pleasant family pet, I whole-heartedly recommend, the purchase of a puppy.

Where adult dogs are concerned, simply ask yourself, 'Would I part with a really good Bull Terrier which meets all my expectations?' For most people, the answer would be 'Certainly not!' If the dog is a fully-integrated member of the family, is loved by everybody and fulfils all your dreams, only the most extreme of circumstances would persuade you to part with it. Fortunately, most dog owners are not prepared to sell an older dog even if it has one or two faults.

Re-housed dogs

Dogs that are offered for sale are often those which have caused trouble or disappointed their owners to such a degree that they wish to be rid of it. Dogs that are offered for sale with the remark 'due to a change of circumstances' are often poor victims of a purchase that was made simply because the owner felt like it at the time and could not cope with the training a dog demands. So-called 'second-hand' dogs often demonstrate bad behaviour patterns and faults which have usually been caused by their owners and have subsequently led to the sale. Unfortunately there are a large number of dogs which experience such a fate more than once and you should be aware of this when considering this type of purchase.

Of course, there are genuine reasons and circumstances which may lead to the sale of a dog. It is down to your good judgement to decide whether the reason the seller gives you is genuine or merely an excuse. I personally believe that the majority of people who sell their dogs due to a change of circumstance are not always honest about their reasons – if only because they are ashamed of their own failure.

Do not misunderstand me – I am not trying to deter you from offering a kind home to a dog which has experienced inadequate training because its owner just did not know enough about such things! In ninety percent of all cases, a dog such as this deserves to be rescued and offered a more suitable home. All I am trying to do is dispel any illusions you might have and to ensure that you are aware that healing the wounds inflicted by an unreasonable owner will take a lot of patience and sensitivity.

Evaluating the older dog

The anatomy of an adult dog is that much easier to evaluate than that of a pup. However, psychological faults may only be detected at a much later stage. A simple example: in 1967 I purchased a seven month old breed bitch from a well-respected kennel in England – it was the fruit of a dream mating! Three experts accompanied me to England, all of whom had been familiar with this breed for many years, and we all considered this bitch to be our 'dream dog'. However, after the hand-over to its new owner, despite proper keeping and care and paying plenty of attention to its small dog personality, the bitch's physical and mental state remained that of the seven month old bitch – even after two litters! It simply failed to develop fully – both physically and mentally.

Nevertheless, it became my children's favourite dog but, for me, the prospect of show success remained just a dream.

The older dog in a new home

My principal recommendation regarding the purchase of an adult dog is to agree a four week trial period. Owners whose only interest is to make money will hesitate to agree to a trial period or decline such an offer altogether. In such a case, I recommend that you do not make the purchase even if the offer is very tempting. Owners who are interested in the welfare of their dog will happily accept a trial period, especially if the buyer is trustworthy, and would prefer to take their dog back rather than see it be unhappy in a new home.

I once, half jokingly, half serious, recommended to the British, with their large number of mass breeders, that they should continue to protect their quarantine regulations (in place because of the risk of rabies). For such measures would certainly ensure that they would not have to take back all the inferior dogs they export so readily; and I was not thinking primarily of Bull Terriers! You may, perhaps, find a comparison with the used car market somewhat strange, but just think – there are excellent used cars and there are also quite a lot of old bangers, in spite of the MOT certificate.

Therefore, if you intend to purchase a dog that is given away due to a 'change of circum-stances', be prepared to look into the matter thoroughly! The dogs, in most cases, deserve a new home, however the buyer may have a frustrating time ahead. According to my own experience, it takes roughly a year for a dog to settle down to its new environment.

BULL TERRIERS IN DISTRESS!

This is not a pleasant topic, but it is one that I feel needs mentioning! Many years ago in England, the Bull Terrier's country of origin, The Bull Terrier Club established a Welfare Fund which accommodates, cares for and arranges re-housing of Bull Terriers which have been maltreated. This serves as an enlightened example to numerous other breed clubs but, unfortunately, it is a necessity in the case of the Bull Terrier.

Bull Terrier Clubs in mainland Europe also take a sympathetic approach to such matters and there are central puppy placing services and an excellent private initiative to help animals in distress. However, it is sad to note how many Bull Terriers have to rely on the support of public and privately-run dog homes. There is a complete lack of suitable professional facilities and, unfortunately, this problem is not tackled by the responsible breed clubs as vigorously as it is by our friends in England.

Why do Bull Terriers in particular need our help?

Very few breeds have been so misunderstood and abused by humans as the Bull Terrier. The legendary reputation of these dogs, their character, determination and courage encourages the wrong type of owners to purchase dogs of this breed. It is not until much later that these people come to realise that they are unable to cope with such a dog.

Such illusions are fuelled by the negative image of these dogs created by the media and by lack-lustre, ill-informed journalists and politicians looking to use the issue for self-promotional means.

Perhaps I should say this one more time: The Bull Terrier is a pleasant, affectionate family pet – a children lover, leisure time companion and a dog that enjoys human company – however, it is also a dog which requires firm and sensible training in order to develop all these positive characteristics to the full.

The much-publicised fighting dog hysteria has no foundation in reality, but can make life difficult for a lot of Bull Terrier owners. The termination of leases on accommodation and disagreements with hysterical neighbours have caused many a Bull Terrier to lose its favourite armchair in the living room. Still, it is only fair to acknowledge that the foolish behaviour and lack of responsibility of a handful of Bull Terrier owners, who fail to train their dogs adequately, support some of these claims. The true victim, as always, is the dog!

The number of Bull Terriers waiting in rescue homes for a new owner to come and claim them is a disgrace for the whole of the community of Bull Terrier friends and an outcry against the breed clubs that are supposed to look after the Bull Terrier! Why don't these clubs charge a nominal fee for each registered puppy which would then contribute to a fund that's sole purpose is to provide new homes for maltreated Bull Terriers? Why are there no tombolas, no charity events, no fund-raising initiatives? At present – and I fear this will remain the same for the foreseeable future – the fate of these dogs lies in the hands of a small group of volunteers who give up their spare time and money to help Bull Terriers in distress.

I appeal to all Bull Terrier friends – please give your support to these volunteers, both

This five month old was awarded the titles 'International Champion' and 'World Champion'. Its body shape conforms to the Standard in all aspects, showing a good head shape and a strong, sturdy body.

This six month old male was awarded the title 'English Champion'. It has a beautiful head with excellent eyes and a well-proportioned, short back, strong bones and excellent angulation.

Bull Terriers of the quality shown above are rarely offered for sale as they are the pride of their owner and breeder.

53

'Bull Royal' – an oil painting by Renaud Ditte.

financially and personally.

If you are intending to purchase a Bull Terrier, don't just visit renowned breed kennels but enquire whether you may find a suitable dog through a rescue centre or a national dog home. You will find the relevant address in the telephone directory.

Selecting a dog from a dog's home

Of course, all the advice relating to

the purchase of an adult dog also applies to a maltreated Bull Terrier. Such a dog will require a great deal of understanding and affection from a dedicated owner. In rare cases, a 'welfare' Bull Terrier may become a glittering show champion. However, you should be content in the knowledge that you are giving a dog a second chance at life in a loving and caring home which is a far cry from its poor start in the hands of unreasonable owners.

Perhaps I can make this decision a little easier by telling you that, in my home country of Germany, a large number of good Bull Terriers have been successfully placed with new owners and that the character of this breed facilitates such a move. In some ways it is as though if the dog experiences a better life then it is quite happy to adjust to its new environment.

Its new owner should not only have good intentions and show due sensitivity, but should also make proper plans and provisions for the introduction of the dog into its new environment. Even when proper training is provided and the dog receives plenty of understanding and affection, you may still experience set backs from time to time. You should not allow this to discourage you, as these phases generally pass if you are patient.

Should you decide to adopt a dog in distress, then you are required to provide a great deal of patience, understanding and persistence – and plenty of time. To feel really comfortable, your dog may need a year, sometimes less, sometimes more, and if you are a dedicated and responsible owner, you should not let this deter you! Visit a dog's home and look at the Bull Terriers housed there. I sincerely hope that you won't be able to resist those sad, pleading eyes.

Chapter Four

THE YOUNG BULL TERRIER

Int. Ch. Abraxas McDayd, four months old.   *Photo: Dr. Fleig.*

TRAINING

The key to successful dog ownership is the provision of consistent training from day one. This basic rule especially applies to the Bull Terrier for these dogs possess a strong will, intelligence and a lot of charm and they also have an inherent tendency to train their owners! It is during the important first few weeks that the decision of who is going to train whom is determined. If you fail to make your intentions quite clear during this phase, you will no doubt find that your Bull Terrier will take the initiative and you will find your life being led by your dog's demands. Getting off to such a bad start will no doubt be difficult and time-consuming to rectify later. Therefore, training should commence the minute you collect your Bull Terrier from the breeder.

Teaching acceptable behaviour
From day one, you should house-train your dog and teach it how to behave properly in your house and in your garden, toward other people and all other creatures for that matter. These first training steps form the basis for your dog's behaviour in later life and so, even though you may feel charmed into submission by your cute little puppy, be firm. There is no need for harsh words or punitive behaviour, in fact you should approach the task of training with a fair amount of affection, but firmness should always be the key element.

Ethologists' studies have clearly established the following:
a) The correct separation age for a puppy is exactly seven weeks.
b) The dog possesses its greatest disposition to learn at an age of between six weeks and four months.

Due to lack of space I am unable to give you all the details of this research, however, I would like to assure my readers that I would not pass on such research findings without first thoroughly checking their validity or having seen them to be true from my own experiences.

With reference to the separation age, Eberhard Trumler – one the most highly-regarded researchers in this field – has determined that in the case of a family of wild dogs where both male dog and bitch rear the puppies, the bitch transfers the further education of her litter to the male after exactly seven weeks; this constitutes a fundamental change in a pup's life. Quite rightly, Trumler concludes from this that it may prove very sensible to transfer the whelp to its new environment at the age of seven weeks, as this corresponds to its natural development.

Early experiences
With regard to this, I would mention again that it is the early experiences which have an enormous impact on the puppy's development and leave life-long impressions. Leaving a puppy with its natural family up to the age of ten or twelve weeks may be recommended if you wish your pup to develop maximum dog-to-dog behaviour patterns. However, our training aims to integrate the dog into our human community as smoothly as possible and it is essential that the puppy can successfully find its place in the mixed human/dog pack to become a fully-integrated member of the family. It is precisely for this reason that I drew your attention to the importance of correct breeding facilities when I discussed selecting a puppy earlier in the

book. A good breeder will promote a puppy's contact with humans from a very young age.

The dog's capacity for learning

Let's now talk about a pup's disposition to learn. Using a modern metaphor, Eberhard Trumler compares the pup's brain with a computer that has not yet been programmed and he underlines the fact that the final programming for the rest of the dog's life takes place within its first four months. All the experiences streaming into its brain during this period go to determine whether or not the dog will become a good member of our human community.

It is important to bear in mind that a young dog will learn constantly during this phase even if you do not teach it anything specific. If you do not employ a tried and tested training formula, your dog's behaviour will be founded upon those things that it encounters each day by pure chance, and such events may not necessarily provide the desired response. These haphazard experiences will then determine your dog's future behaviour for life!

Train your Bull Terrier to be ready to learn from its early days. If you present a training routine to your dog as a new game and a new experience everyday, it will be more than willing to learn. Take the time to programme this young brain, for this is the way to produce a dog that will cause very few problems and bring a lot of joy and pleasure to you and your family.

The awareness of a dog's great capacity to learn during this early phase has produced a completely new basis for the training of dogs over the last twenty years. However, a large number of authors and trainers have failed to instigate this new thinking and write or learn from out-dated books. Should you wish to refer to a printed guide to training your dog, you should ensure that you choose one which embraces this modern research or seek out training methods such as those of

We're ready for training now!   Photo: G. Michel.

the American, Richard A. Wolters. Wolters is a very intelligent hound trainer who baffled the rather conservative hunting community with the fact that his working hounds can produce excellent results in a hunting environment by the age of seven to ten months. His training methods are as successful as they are revolutionary and are based on the research of American ethologists which, in turn, reflect Eberhard Trumler's findings.

Perhaps I may also mention the British ethologist Roger Mugford who uses exactly the same findings as a basis and has written a book which outlines the behaviour of disturbed dogs. Such a book gives a valuable insight into dog behaviour and is worth reading whether your dog is disturbed or not.

The basis for a Bull Terrier puppy's training is consistency combined with a good basic knowledge of dog behaviour and training. If you start at the age of seven weeks, you will be rewarded with a well-trained family pet by the age of 16 to 22 weeks.

Avoiding injury

Still, I would like to mention the following specifically with regard to the training of a Bull Terrier. When the pup arrives at your home, it comes complete with a set of small, shiny razor-sharp teeth and it will have already learned to use these to best effect during play with its brothers and sisters. However, your dog has no idea how sensitive human skin is, compared to the tougher nature of a dog's coat. There are several ways to deal with this problem; for example, you could take to wearing leather gloves when playing with the new arrival. However, it is far more sensible to make the pup aware that its teeth

can cause pain to humans and to teach it to be more gentle, particularly when playing with children. In the litter, your puppy's sisters and brothers will have fought back when hurt and so should you. Warn it very gently and, in this way, your puppy will soon come to understand that it is causing pain. I specifically chose this particular problem as it is one which often creates misunderstandings. Bull Terrier puppies are rough diamonds and it is necessary to counteract any adverse behaviour immediately, maintaining a gentle but firm approach.

PROVIDING A SUITABLE HOME

The most basic provision for your dog is a place of its own within your home, where it can retreat to. A dog such as the Bull Terrier revels in human company and so the selected spot should be in a much-used part of the home from where your dog can still feel your presence but, at the same time, rest conveniently out of the way. It is vital for a young dog to have a special place which is entirely its own territory. Many owners opt for buying a special wicker basket for this purpose and young dogs love these all the more as they also provide an opportunity to try out their teeth!

Because of this tendency, I would recommend an indoor dog kennel which has a robust cage construction and a lockable front. These often have a solid chipboard or metal base which can be lined with old towels or bedding; your dog will really appreciate being able to dig around in these to create its own bed. Many of these also fold flat making them suitable for use when travelling or on car trips.

Most dog owners appear to

have a rather distorted idea of such a kennel and do not wish to lock up their dog under any circumstances. However, I guess it has slipped their minds that dogs in the wild used to live in burrows with walls all around and a cover on top to give them a feeling of security. All dogs love burrows – even if they come in the form of a portable kennel. When choosing a suitable kennel, the cage varieties are often preferable as these allow air to circulate freely – bear in mind that dogs need more oxygen than we do.

House training

During its first months, a lockable sleeping box may prove particularly helpful in house-training as a dog will rarely soil its bed. Because of this, the cage can be used as an effective tool when tackling this issue.

When providing house-training for a puppy, try to stick to a few basic rules: Take your pup outside to its toilet as soon as it wakes up, after meals and if the pup becomes agitated in any way. After just one to two weeks, you should find that your puppy has a firm grasp of the notion of toilet training.

The lockable sleeping kennel has another advantage in that it can keep your pet out of harm's way for short periods of time. During its first few months, a young dog can cause a fair amount of damage and all because it can't resist trying out those sharp little teeth on any accessible object. Table legs, carpets, cables – none of these things are safe from the young Bull Terrier's enthusiastic fangs. This can end up costing you a fortune but, on a more important note, it can also constitute a risk to your dog's health. If, during the day, you need to pop out to the

shops for ten minutes or, for some reason, can't keep a close eye on your Bull Terrier for a period up to an hour, you may insist that your puppy takes a compulsory nap safe inside its sleeping kennel. Don't get me wrong – I am not recommending that you lock your pet up for long periods of time on a regular basis. I have had the misfortune to come across Bull Terrier owners who keep their wards like battery chickens and this is a terrible cruelty to inflict on an animal such as this. As long as a Bull Terrier has ample opportunity to establish and maintain a close relationship with its human companions, the occasional enforced nap here or there will not cause any great harm.

Access to areas out of doors

So long as sufficient exercise is provided, these dogs do not object to living in a small flat. However, all dogs appreciate access to a garden if possible as this provides additional opportunities for running around. A word of warning, though – your garden must be fitted with a suitably secure fence. In principal, the dog's place is really at the side of its owner at all times, although the garden can provide an additional exciting environment so long as the owner is sensible about protecting flower beds and vegetable plots from the curiosity of his or her four-legged friend. You should train your dog to use a dedicated toilet area in your garden, keeping the majority of the garden free from any unpleasant fouling.

Taking part is everything for us humans and we all enjoy the challenge of new and fresh experiences. The same applies to your dog and you should endeavour to offer it a new experience every day of its life. The more diverse and colourful its environment, the more opportunity your dog will have to learn new things.

Setting the boundaries

Your Bull Terrier will enjoy accompanying you throughout all aspects of your daily life. However, this can be taken too far and I fully support dog owners who draw the line at allowing their pet to sleep in their bed. There are very few other dog breeds which are so strongly drawn to the human bed or cosy sofa than the Bull Terrier, after all, it just loves to snuggle into any cosy spot it finds. Nevertheless, you should insist on creating certain areas which are out of bounds for your dog and you will have to stick to this rule quite firmly and persistently. Eventually, your dog will get the message and respect your decision, but be prepared for it to try every which way to overthrow your decision on this count.

I don't see any problem with allowing your dog to have its own armchair or a dedicated area on the sofa. You can place a blanket on the designated area and this will not only protect the furniture, but can be helpful in signalling to your dog that this spot belongs to him, but the rest of the furniture is for you alone. Why do dogs yearn to be up on the sofa? All dogs like to watch the world from the highest vantage point available!

VISITING THE OUTSIDE WORLD

As soon as it has had all its necessary protective vaccinations, your Bull Terrier can accompany you in the outside world as you go about your day to day business. Take your dog wherever you go, not just to green areas for exercise, but to the town with all

its noise and traffic. You should aim to familiarise your dog with a wide selection of environments from an early age and the same is true for car journeys. By making car trips from an early age, your dog is less likely to fall prey to travel sickness.

To begin with, the journeys should be kept short and it is advisable to make these early journeys to open green areas where your dog can exercise and relieve itself. In this way, your dog will equate the car trip with an enjoyable destination and come to see the car as a means to fun.

When visiting the town, it is recommended that you carry your pup now and then to give it ample opportunity to study the busy environment and become used to the various noises. In the city, you should keep your dog on a lead as this is a compulsory safety requirement. Therefore, collar and lead training should be given from an early age.

Should your puppy display a fear of an object or situation it encounters, take time to familiarise it with this. Patience is called for in this situation to avoid putting your dog under any unnecessary pressure and to allay the fear successfully. Your dog must have complete faith that no harm will come to it while you are around.

Exercise for the puppy

While young, your puppy may tire easily and you may not always notice this. It upsets me to see three or four month old pups being dragged for hours across show grounds by their oblivious owners. Total exhaustion can seriously damage the health of your dog and the constant bombardment of new impressions coupled with the puppy's natural instinct to follow its owner may conceal such physical

Bull Terriers love close contact with humans.

Photo: Helga Döbrentey.

The Bull Terrier's great affection for children should be maintained and proper training will ensure that play is safe. However, you should always supervise such activities. *Photo: Mehringer.*

tiredness. When exercising your puppy, remember less is more – your young dog will certainly be more appreciative of five or six shorter walks as opposed to one giant marathon. For a four month old puppy, twenty minutes is adequate. At five months, the time span rises to thirty minutes and the time length can be gradually increased as your dog grows older.

When you watch dogs at play with their own kind, you will notice how lively and exciting their play can be. After a period of time, the play slows down and this is when it should be brought to an end. In order to develop properly, a young dog requires plenty of rest to allow for healthy growth and so your puppy will demand an adequate amount of sleep.

Try to encourage as much contact as possible between your Bull Terrier and people, children and other pets during its first year. This contact should be supervised to ensure that your dog does not get carried away by all the excitement. However interesting and attractive all these new experiences are for your dog, it must quickly learn that it is its master or mistress who determines when play time is over and that it is its duty to follow his or her commands.

Balancing the character

Every animal possesses aggressive tendencies as well as fears and, during its first year, your dog must learn to control both. Adequate patience and firm handling, along with some affectionate sensitivity on your part, will smooth the way to your dog developing a balanced character. You should never try to rush this – patience will allow your dog to come to realise that its fears are unfounded. Putting pressure on a scared dog along

with negative experiences may cause long term psychological damage and should be avoided at all costs. Frightening noises or confrontations will lose their power if the dog is allowed to gradually become familiar with them.

If your dog displays aggressive behaviour, this can be overcome with effective training. During the time when the pup is still with its littermates, a responsible breeder will intervene if a play fight gets out of control and will take action to discourage the puppies from taking their play to such extremes. A bitch with good maternal instincts will do exactly the same to keep her brood in order.

Maintaining control

The Bull Terrier is, perhaps, the least suitable breed for anti-authoritarian training regimes. A gentle smack if it is well-deserved and the occasional shake if the pup is really out of control are quite sensible training measures. What you should not encourage, however, are those games which promote aggressive behaviour such as tug of war games in which the toy is not released. I am thinking mainly of the game that involves a piece of sack or a stick. A hound may sink its teeth into such an item and refuse to let go. Pulling at a rope is certainly good exercise but, with a Bull Terrier, you must always remember that all such games should be ended by the master's command so that the dog never gets the opportunity to conclude that it is the stronger party. For this to be successful, you must train your dog to release an object on command. This type of training will also prove useful in retrieval games such as fetching a ball or stick. Your dog will thoroughly enjoy such games and can be encouraged to retrieve all manner of objects. However, you must always ensure that such objects are large enough not to constitute any risk of swallowing.

The rebellious phase

When training your dog, it is important to bear in mind that, like humans, most dogs will go through a rebellious phase when they reach puberty. You will notice the first of these phases at ten months of age and another again at twenty months as the dog reaches true adulthood. Appropriate firm handling and sensible training should quell any mutinous tendencies and your Bull Terrier should return to its usual congenial self after two to three weeks.

Of course, there will always be the occasional individual who insists on trying it on just that little bit harder, and you should be warned that such dogs may even resort to snarling or snapping at those family members which it deems to be below it in the pack hierarchy. Such attacks should not be tolerated and this sort of behaviour justifies a good slap to keep the errant teenager in order. Less resolute masters or mistresses should take heed – if this type of behaviour is ignored or not firmly discouraged immediately, the dog will continue to make such aggressive attacks and the problem will escalate. In view of this, you should take firm, positive action at the first signs of such behaviour to let your dog know that this will simply not be tolerated.

Achieving a good temperament

In this context, I cannot remain silent on the fact that in some breed kennels, where the focus is on show success alone, an aggressive or shy temperament is still often accepted in order to achieve an anatomical ideal such as the perfect head form. Litters from dog families which have an unstable temperament may even be considered dangerous during their teen phase and so, for this reason, it is important to ensure that the dog of your choice comes from a well-balanced line. If you cannot judge this for yourself, ask an expert for some guidance and don't take the risk of buying a pup if there is any risk of behavioural problems developing later. A number of Bull Terriers have attacked family members during this phase and have had to be put down as a result. Remember, no matter how beautiful a dog may be, your first responsibility must be to safeguard the health and safety of your family.

Throughout the first year of a Bull Terrier's life, a sensible owner will do everything in his or her power to establish a harmonious relationship with the dog, showing lots of affection, giving an endless string of cuddles and promoting the puppy's desire to learn in a playful manner. Each day embraces new experiences and brings joy and pleasure both to the owner and the dog. A young Bull Terrier will truly enrich its owner's life.

PROVIDING A SUITABLE DIET

The aggressive approach of advertising for the dog food industry would have us believe that, thanks to the comprehensive range of foods provided by large multi-nationals, the issue of providing a suitable, balanced diet for your dog has been thoroughly resolved; indeed, there is a wide range of proven, excellent dog foods available. However, the responsible dog owner needs to take a selective and well-informed approach to the subject of diet.

Ethologists have often been quoted as saying that dogs are not particularly fussy about what they eat and I find this most amazing. You can test the validity of such statements yourself by serving your dog a piece of meat, a piece of cheese, a banana, an apple, a cooked potato and a piece of bread. You will find that such a test will throw up a number of different reactions. All of my Bull Terriers have had a fondness for particular sorts of treats. If you take a critical look at the Bull Terrier, it would seem that its sturdy structure gives the impression that such a dog would like the idea of good, substantial meals. Some advertising campaigns suggest that you should fill your dog's bowl with a sufficient quantity of complete dog food and allow it to pick at this as and when it feels like it. Others recommend a wide range of tinned foods containing a selection of meat derivatives such as beef, chicken, game, heart, liver and rabbit. Perhaps I am a little old-fashioned in my approach. Of course I take advantage of processed convenience foods, but I choose to supplement these with carefully selected fresh ingredients to make my dogs' diet more varied and tasty. Your dog's requirements will alter at various stages throughout its life. Below you will find a suitable feeding schedule for puppies.

Feeding schedule for eight week old Bull Terrier puppies
8-20 weeks
Four meals a day.

Breakfast –
Standard breakfast cereal, brown bread or puppy meal in warm, unboiled 3.5% fat milk with an added tablespoon of full fat puppy milk powder. This can be sweetened with a little honey and half a grated apple. Twice a week a fresh raw egg should be added to the mixture.

Lunch –
10-15g (½oz) meat for each week of the puppy's age added to wholemeal puppy meal soaked in gravy or meat broth. Cut raw meat into small pieces and feed warm. Calcium and vitamin supplements should be added to this meal along with a portion of grated vegetables such as carrot, cauliflower, spinach and peas.

Tea –
A milk pudding, egg custard or the same as breakfast, adding a little malt extract.

Supper –
The same as lunch. Vary the type of meal given, both cooked and raw. In place of one of the meat meals you can also offer the following alternatives: 1 boiled or scrambled egg; 25-50g (1-2oz) grated cheese moistened with a little raw egg or milk; fish, rabbit, well-boned chicken, tripe – raw or cooked.

In addition 5ml (one teaspoon) of cod liver oil should be given. This can be licked off the spoon, sweetened with some sugar or there are varieties avilable which can be mixed with food. A strong marrow bone can also be provided under supervision, but bones which splinter should not be offered.

Nutritional supplements
Most ready-prepared dog food mixtures already contain all the necessary vitamins and minerals. However, you must ensure that an adolescent Bull Terrier receives sufficient vitamins and minerals according to the food manufacturer's instructions. The

quantities of food listed in the diet here is an average and you will find that feeding requirements vary from dog to dog. The basic rule of thumb is that your dog should eat the whole portion of food served within five minutes and, after this period, any leftovers should be discarded. Under no circumstances should the dog be allowed to help itself to left overs or any other source of food in between meals, as this encourages poor eating habits.

Do not let an obstinate dog dictate its own diet as this produces a picky eater. For instance, your dog may decide that it would prefer more meat in the morning rather than the milk meal. This should not be allowed as the diet is formulated to provide balanced nutrition. You may, however, supplement the milk food with yoghurt or a low-fat curd cheese and you should try to introduce a wide variety of meats in the evening meal – tinned foods are available in a wide range of flavours. Do not spoil your dog – make it quite clear that you expect it to eat whatever you put in front of it. Leftovers should not be reused once they have been served to the dog but, if you have prepared too much food, you may store the excess in the refrigerator and then reheat it and serve it the next day.

The growing dog

As the puppy grows older, you should reduce the number of meals served per day. The first reduction is made at the age of three to four months when the tea meal is discontinued and the supper meal brought forward to 7.00pm to compensate. By the age of seven months, only two meals should be served per day – the milk meal in the morning and the meat meal in the evening at 7.00pm. Vitamin supplements and mineral mixtures along with the cod liver oil is served up until the age of approximately fifteen months, providing that any tinned foods served are not vitamin and mineral enriched.

You must take care when giving additional supplements to your dog as too much can be as harmful as a deficiency.

To strengthen the jaws and teeth, strong marrow bones can be given but you should guard against giving too many bones as this can result in hard motions and your dog may also lose its appetite. The gnawing of bones is primarily a pleasant occupation for your dog and they do not really constitute food as such. Never give your dog pork or chicken bones to gnaw as these are brittle and are likely to splinter into slivers which can cause damage to the larynx, stomach or bowel. Beef bones are a more suitable choice and will keep your dog occupied for some time.

A dog breed such as the Bull Terrier grows very quickly and will reach its adult height by the age of nine months. Therefore, you need to ensure that it receives excellent nutrition up to this age to cope with this spurt of growth. Quality of food is extremely important, more so than quantity. Avoid over-feeding your dog and allowing it to become overweight – you should always be able to detect individual ribs on a properly fed Bull Terrier. The correct balance between diet and exercise is vital to keep your dog in optimum health.

Creating good habits

Picky eaters are made not born and, if there are no other signs of illness or disease, you can ignore the occasional bout of poor appetite which often indicates a natural regulation of food intake after a large meal. Dog owners who become over-anxious about their pet's eating habits – worrying about whether the dog is eating too little or too much – often create the effect they are trying to avoid. It is far more advisable to show patience and tolerance. I have seen cases in which over-anxious owners take all the pleasure out of meal times for their dogs. Such nervousness may be attributed to the slightly misleading phrase in the Standard which stipulates that the Bull Terrier should possess maximum substance. As discussed earlier,

Ringo and Marco enjoy a sprint! A properly-trained Bull Terrier makes an excellent playmate! Photo: Klaus Bartsch.

in this instance, substance is primarily an anatomical feature and is not achieved by over-feeding.

Keeping your dog trim

Unfortunately, a large number of show judges, along with a great many owners, have not seen the issue of substance in its true light and this may be why you will find suggestions that a dog should be fed extra food for the six weeks prior to a show. In my opinion, this is total nonsense! Stick with the basic rules – the ribs should be detectable and a Bull Terrier should have a clearly defined waistline as shown in the pictures which illustrate the Standard in Chapter Two. Remember, obesity is a threat to your dog's health and a slimmer dog will be far fitter.

Many Bull Terriers are real food addicts and you may have to exercise some willpower on your dog's behalf. These days, the pet food industry produces special diet food to help reduce your dog's weight and you shouldn't hesitate to use this if it becomes necessary. The carrying of extra weight not only looks unappealing and is bad for the dog's health, but it also makes the dog lazy and apathetic. Moderation in all things is an excellent maxim and sadly one that is rarely applied these days.

EXERCISE AND GAMES

The Bull Terrier is one of the rare breeds of dog that adapts happily to living in moderate residential environments. However, in this situation, you must pay particular attention to the provision of adequate exercise which is necessary to work the legs and muscles and also to stimulate the dog's senses. At larger kennels in England, the kennel maid is

required to walk each dog, on the lead, across roads and fields for a distance of three kilometres (two miles). This is known as road walking and is introduced to the dog from the age of six months. Such a walk is particularly important for a kennel dog which does not get the opportunity to get sufficient exercise otherwise.

In recent years, the development of the flexible 'adventure' lead, with its automatic roll-out/up and quick stop facilities and extension length of 5-8m (5½-9yds) has been a real bonus. This allows our four-legged friend the maximum freedom on a lead and yet it remains within an adequate control range. Of course freedom off the lead is even more fun for the dog as this allows the most opportunity to use its senses to the full, sniffing out new and interesting things.

How much and how often?

Aim to provide three half hour long walks each day and a longer walk of maybe two to three hours at the weekend to keep your Bull Terrier fit and lively. This should be easy to achieve in rural areas but, for city-based dogs, you may have to adapt this routine to ensure your dog receives adequate exercise.

Introducing suitable toys

Playing games can help to strengthen muscles and the cardio-vascular system and retrieving games can be a great source of entertainment for the dog, although not all Bull Terriers are fond of such activities. Teach your dog to retrieve objects from an early age. Avoid small objects and balls smaller than the size of a tennis ball as there is always the danger that such an object may become stuck deep in the dog's throat. Stones should never be used as they cause damage to the teeth and you should take care when selecting sticks as rough wood can also cause injury. There are a number of specialist dog toys available on the market which are both safe and fun to use.

Toys such as the Boomer Ball are particularly favoured by Bull Terriers. These balls are too large for the dog to grasp with its teeth and this encourages the dog to dribble with the ball using its head and body instead. Boomer Balls are perfectly safe because there is no risk of swallowing them and their hard rubber construction makes them durable and difficult to destroy. The larger balls, with a diameter of 25cm (10in) can be filled with sand or small pebbles to give additional weight and those filled with pebbles have the added advantage of creating a particular sound which can all add to the fun for your dog.

Another favourite toy with Bull Terriers Is the Kong – a solid rubber dancing toy. No matter how you throw the Kong, it jumps unpredictably from one spot to another. This unpredictable behaviour results from its unusual construction. In contrast to the normal rubber ball, the Kong makes 90 degree wrenches and turns which makes retrieving it that bit more of a challenge. It is available in several forms – the red which has a particularly strong springing action and the black which is extra durable and tough enough to stand up to even a Bull Terrier's teeth! Toys such as these have been used as therapeutic aids in treating caged animals which lack sufficient stimulation.

A word of warning – when playing these sorts of games, you must teach your Bull Terrier to release the toy on command from an early age. Toys which fit into your dog's mouth and can be encased by its teeth will be impossible to remove otherwise, especially if your dog has set its heart on keeping hold of it. This may then result in a long and laborious chase which will no doubt be great fun for your dog, but not so much fun for you.

On unpleasant, rainy days, you can use toys to keep your Bull Terrier occupied indoors, but you will have to ensure that the play does not get too rowdy and that furniture and breakable household objects are not likely to be damaged. A Bull Terrier needs constant stimulation of its senses and work for its teeth and this is exactly what these toys can provide.

Other suitable activities
Sometimes a look at what is happening with other breeds can do no harm at all and may bring a fresh perspective. In the case of hound training, a retriever becomes passionate about retrieving and sees this activity as a constantly stimulating and interesting game. The dog handler will use specially developed dummies for retrieving and may even employ a dummy launcher which is capable of launching the object over longer distances. If you are interested in involving your dog in retrieval work, there are several specialist books available which detail training methods or you might even consider enrolling in some classes.

Working Dog trials also contain some interesting features such as the retrieve buck which is available in various different weight categories according to your dog's size. Some retrieve bucks have facilities which allow for the attachment or removal of additional weights. Once your Bull Terrier has successfully mastered this game with the retrieve buck, with good training it should be able to achieve excellent retrieving results. The wide range of items that can be used in retrieval games keep these activities interesting for your dog and such games provide a useful form of exercise to keep your dog fit and lively.

Another wonderful game that your dog is sure to enjoy is hide and seek. This game tests all of the Bull Terrier's senses. You can introduce this game to your dog during a walk in the park or woods. When your dog has found something to capture its interest and is otherwise occupied, you should hide behind a tree or a bush. Your dog will have great fun searching for you. If you are out walking with a friend, you can set up a mini trail for your dog to follow. Your friend should keep your dog on its lead while you head off out of sight. Your dog can then follow this trail to find you, and the reunion which follows is always a cause of great excitement. Such exercises can form a good basis for future, more advanced trailing work.

Games are a lot of fun for both dogs and their owners and provide an interesting alternative to the limited homelife that a family pet usually experiences. These activities broaden the dog's horizons and strengthen the bond between the dog and its human companions.

THE BULL TERRIER AND OTHER ANIMALS

I have already emphasised the importance of contact between dog and humans when discussing the correct age of separation of the puppy from the litter. Many young dogs have a fair bit of catching up to do with regard to proper dog to dog behaviour. If the pup has stayed with its mother and litter mates up to the age of twelve weeks, it will have had the opportunity to develop a better understanding of the dog pack hierarchy, behaviour patterns of its own kind and, not least, the individual dog language.

Mixing with other dogs

Most pups, being separated from the litter at seven weeks old, lack these early experiences and this can lead to confrontations when the teenager or adult dog is allowed off the leash and encounters strange dogs. In Britain, many dog clubs hold meetings several times a week where young and old dogs of all breeds can come together with their owners. Such an activity is recommended as it gives a dog ample opportunity to mix with its own kind and develop a better understanding of dog behaviour. In these situations, it is the owner's responsibility to ensure that his or her dog is well-behaved and that there are no nasty confrontations or aggressive behaviour. Don't be alarmed if a rude, frolicsome young dog is firmly put in its place by an elder – after all, this is the whole point of bringing a young dog to such meetings. It would be totally wrong to carry a young dog around in your arms, protecting it from larger dogs as this would deny it the opportunity to learn how to react to everyday situations. By attending dog club meetings and allowing your Bull Terrier to find its place in the dog world, you will soon see that your dog actually enjoys such encounters.

However, if your dog is overly-aggressive or extremely shy, it may be unsuitable to take to a club meeting. Such dogs have a tendency to create negative reactions and may actually do

One of the most important training tasks is aimed at establishing a good relationship with all other animals. Fausto fell in love with the hump geese and they fell in love with him. The expression of affection, in this case, involved a gentle embrace of the goose's neck by the dog's fangs.

Photos: Verene Höchner.

psychological harm to themselves or the other dogs that they meet. A dog club will usually employ an experienced dog expert who will oversee the meet and who has the authority to exclude unsuitable participants from the group.

Meeting other animals

Creating a social meeting for your Bull Terrier with other dogs is one thing, however, introducing it to other types of animal is quite another. The Bull Terrier's natural tendency to show aggressive behaviour toward larger animals such as cows, horses and elephants may be attributed to its almost-diminished fighting dog ancestry. I have often made a point of taking my own dogs to dog-friendly zoos and farms to help familiarise them with these more unusual creatures.

Early contact with all manner of house and farm animals such as cats, budgies, chicken and geese is vital for the dog's development and lessens the friction when these animals are encountered again at a later age. It may take a

little patience and practise, but all Bull Terriers have the capacity to learn to respect other animals and, in some cases, a deep and lasting friendship can develop. Just look at these photographs of Fausto and the hump geese. One goose fell so much in love with my Bull Terrier that it failed to develop the normal amorous feelings toward the males of its own species and remained ever-faithful to Fausto.

The wonderful Bull Terrier makes a trusty companion for every dog lover and, at the same time, offers a highly interesting training challenge to those who take their responsibility as a dog owner seriously. As an owner, the worst thing you can do for yourself and your dog is to waste the opportunity of developing a good, respectful relationship between the two of you. Make good use of your Bull Terrier's first year when it is at its most keen and receptive. Take the time and dedication to achieve an excellent integration of your Bull Terrier into your family and, indeed, the human community as a whole.

Chapter Five

THE ADULT BULL TERRIER

It's a dog's life!

FAMILY LIFE

There are very few breeds of dog of this size that adapt to the human family so harmoniously as the Bull Terrier. However, this transition does require some human effort and proper training is essential.

As I mentioned earlier, many Bull Terrier owners are avid fans of the breed and will sing their praises with abundant enthusiasm at any given opportunity. Well, it is difficult not to fall in love with such an adorable sweet-natured dog! In short: 'Once an owner of a Bull Terrier, always an owner of a Bull Terrier!' and you will find this to be true of most owners that you may encounter. I personally can vouch for the fact that these dogs deserve such lavish appreciation!

However, let me give you a word of warning – Bull Terriers tend to be obstinate and bursting with charm and it is this charm, with all its clownish behaviour, that we fall for ever so readily and ever so often.

Some Bull Terrier owners fail to notice how the training takes a turn and how the dog, bit by bit, begins to train the owner! In the case of many – too many – Bull Terriers, characteristics which are regarded as faults in other breeds are played down, tolerated, put in a different perspective or even glorified. If you look at a three year old Bull Terrier which has experienced proper and successful training during its first year, you will no doubt feel tempted to pay your respects – it has found a way to use its charm and obstinacy to get its own way.

You should not think of this as a tragedy – in fact, smile! As I have said before, this is not a dog for wooden working dog fanatics or irrational people. With the Bull Terrier a good sense of humour is highly recommended, if not a must!

Problems within the family

On many occasions we have been confronted with the concerns of expectant parents who are fretting that problems may arise when the newborn, two-legged family member arrives. 'Would it not be better to give the dog away now?' we are asked. Equally, I have frequently come across the idea that keeping a dog is not appropriate when the children are still too young to understand their responsibilities and that they should reach an acceptable level of responsibility before a dog is introduced to the family.

In some ways, the above ideas and concerns may appear to be logical. However, in the case of the Bull Terrier, they simply do not apply. I already had the pleasure of introducing this breed to you as a true children lover and would mention that my own children and grandchildren, who learned to walk with the dog around, always appeared quite Bull Terrier confident even at a very early age.

It is important that the dog is not reduced to playing second fiddle when a new baby arrives. It should maintain its position as a well-loved family member that is respected by everybody. This is Eberhard Trumler's advice; 'Introduce the baby to the dog as soon as you bring it home from the hospital. We do something very similar when we introduce a young pup as a new companion to our Bull Terrier. Ideally, your Bull Terrier should be present when you change the diapers.'

Another recommendation from Eberhard Trumler – 'The dog should be allowed to sniff at the child's bottom and lick it – for this is typical dog behaviour which establishes a firm and friendly

A new baby has arrived! If introduced correctly, the Bull Terrier will become an affectionate nanny. Photo: H. and M. Krüger.

Adult Bull Terriers make excellent playmates. Photo: Bimmermann.

relationship. Once is enough, just to welcome it – that is quite sufficient.' If the thought of this makes you squeamish, you may always use soap and a sponge afterwards, for the sake of hygiene.

If the baby is given a bottle, do not hesitate to give the remainder to the Bull Terrier as a reward for watching. Very soon a close relationship will be established and many dogs will guard a pram as though their own pups were asleep in it. However – a word of warning – do not leave the Bull Terrier and your baby unsupervised. For there is always the danger that the Bull Terrier's affection for the little fellow may be so great that it will crawl into the child's bed or pram and this will be a step too far for even the strongest of babies.

Occasionally our Bull Terriers will have to put up with quite a lot in their role of 'nanny'. Ears may be used as teething-rings, the tail may be yanked and pulled at now and then and, as the child grows older, the dog may find itself stuffed into the doll's pram and pushed around and about! Very few breeds will so readily and patiently endure this much! The Bull Terrier is difficult to exasperate and is hardly ever grouchy – it loves children. However, unruly children and a Bull Terrier may not make such a harmonious partnership and it is vital that you protect your dog from badly-behaved children. Bull Terriers may have nerves of steel, but have you ever witnessed just what children are capable of doing to animals? You need to bring a certain amount of common sense to the relationship with a little give and take on both sides. Children and dogs tend to train one another and can build up a strong and trusting relationship but you should still never leave them unsupervised!

LEISURE TIME

I have already discussed the exercising requirements of a young Bull Terrier in an earlier chapter. The section featuring games offered some advice on what you and your Bull Terrier can do together – remember, playing is an education for your dog!

There is a wonderful leisure activity called 'agility' and this gives dogs and their owners alike the opportunity to demonstrate their sporting capabilities. Climbing over hurdles, slalom races, crawling through tubes – and all carried out against both the clock and other competitors! The Bull Terrier will enjoy such exercises and competitions very much indeed. However, you should not make successful completion of the tasks compulsory, but rather train your dog to see these competitions as an opportunity to play!

Do not be too keen or expect great results. There are breeds of dog which have had characteristics specially developed for these types of activities, such as the Border Collie or German Shepherd breeds and, participating owners of such breeds will usually achieve top marks easily. Our Bull Terriers take part honouring the saying 'It is not the winning, but the taking part that counts!' And I can assure you that this is great fun and improves both you and your dog's fitness as well.

There are other activities suitable for the Bull Terrier, with one being the quite demanding but very interesting training as a hound. Perhaps even more attractive is the training of your dog as a rescue dog and such special training will offer you years crammed with exciting activities and challenges.

The top model!

Photo: Pete Dine.

Remember to train your Bull Terrier yourself – you should never entrust this important process to a third party! If you do not know how to train your dog, there are courses in almost all areas which you can attend along with your dog and these can be a very enjoyable experience.

Training a dog to be a guard dog has been greeted with increasing disapproval and criticism from the public. The majority of people are asking themselves whether, with the exception of police, military and working dog owners, a private person should be allowed to train his dog to attack another person for whatever reason. This guide, of course, does not provide enough space to discuss this in detail.

With regard to our Bull Terriers, I would however like to mention that I consider the theory that such work would give these former fighting dogs an alternative to their past activities to be total nonsense. To show hostility toward humans would be out of character for a Bull Terrier and to encourage it to do so would be irresponsible. This view is quite rightly backed by the authorities and parliament and, in some countries, even the legal system. I feel confident that I can approach this matter with insight and knowledge as I have actively pursued working dog activities for many years, including those involving the Bull Terrier.

Training a Bull Terrier to attack another person (known as 'man-training') can no longer be justified these days and the risks involved are far too great. I expressly appreciate that clubs promoting dog sports activities generally exclude the Bull Terrier from training as a guard dog.

The tasks that you would normally ask of your Bull Terrier should not require any training as a guard dog. In its land of origin, this has never been encouraged and yet still the Bull Terrier has proved that it is capable of protecting property and family time and time again. The Bull Terrier has an image of being a fierce protector of the home and, in criminal circles, the feeling is that people with Bull Terriers are best left alone. So, what more could you wish for?

HOLIDAYS

Unfortunately, our lifestyle today robs us of the opportunity to spend as much time with our Bull Terrier, as we would no doubt wish to do. Work and other commitments take us away from home or, at the very least, leave us distracted. However, holidays are the times of the year for bringing the whole family together and, of course, our Bull Terrier is a fully recognised member of the family.

The introduction highlights the fact that I do not have much regard for dog owners who put their pets in kennels while they are on holiday. However, if you are travelling to a country which has strict quarantine regulations which do not permit you to take your dog with you, or your choice of holiday comprises of an endless string of sight-seeing tours, then you may have no alternative but to make use of such an establishment. But this then begs the question: 'Why are you not planning a holiday that suits everybody including your dog?' Bringing a dog into your family carries a great deal of responsibility – I have not heard of any attractive 'single holidays' for neglected Bull Terriers.

Boarding kennels
However, in all fairness, sometimes, even with the most careful planning and good

A high long jump!

Photo: G. Barth.

The 'mouse' jump!

Photo: Verena Höchner.

intentions, a boarding kennel is the only option. Placing your dog in a good kennel requires some forward planning as you will need to be sure that you have selected a suitable establishment and this will initially require visits to numerous kennels. Also, you will need to book early to ensure a place in the kennel of your choice, particularly at peak season. The placing of a Bull Terrier brings along its own unique problems. This breed requires individual care and a lot of attention so you will find the quest for a suitable kennel more of a challenge than for most other breeds. The accommodation of Bull Terriers in kennels together with other dogs should be avoided under all circumstances – the Bull Terrier requires its own box and individual care. Bringing Bull Terriers together with other dogs entails risks that I would never consider.

Alternative care arrangements

If possible, you should seek out an alternative solution. Maybe a friend, relative or neighbour who is familiar with your dog and has sufficient time and experience to care for it can look after your dog while you are away. If you are a member of a breed club, then maybe a fellow member can fulfil this role with you offering the same service in return. However, at the end of the day, the best solution for all involved is to take your Bull Terrier on holiday with you.

Just think about how much you'd fret if you had to leave your dog behind. Pangs of guilt and concern over whether your dog is pining for you are not conducive to the most relaxing of holidays. And just think of the fun you can have with your dog during this time – would you really want to be missing out on this?

VETERANS

For a long time, the longevity of life was one of the breeding objectives of responsible Bull Terrier fanciers. Many shows feature special veteran categories which give participants the opportunity to demonstrate the health and freshness of the older Bull Terrier. Unfortunately, today's breeders have abandoned this important breeding objective and it often seems that head profiles are more important than good health in old age.

Still, I believe the average life expectancy of a Bull Terrier to be ten years which is quite normal for a breed of this size and substance. You should refer to Chapter eight of this book for health care advice and, when purchasing a puppy, make sure that its ancestors reached a good age and demonstrated physical and mental fitness in their later years.

A dog for life – that is probably the wish of everyone who buys a puppy. Unfortunately, the life expectancy of humans and dogs is not compatible but, even still, we would like them to be with us for as long as possible!

Modern medicine has gone some way to reduce the effects of age-related ailments in dogs as well as in their owners. However, our four-legged friends have an advantage! If the extension of life means continuous misery with no chance of recovery, we may step in and put an end to the pain and suffering. The administration of an injection can make all pain go away permanently. Many dog owners have had to make the terrible decision that, when there is nothing left that can be done for their pet, the kindest option for the animal is to call in the vet. I have had to face this myself and I know

The Bull Terrier is a smart dog.   *Photo: Arno Santner.*

Swimming and retrieving is fun!

The Bull Terrier retains its freshness in old age! Int. Ch. Abraxax McDayd (Cäsar) at 12 years of age. Photo: Dr. Fleig.

Amanda von der Vogelweide, 15 years old. Photo: Lotte Frank.

how hard it is to make this call but, thanks to this, our dogs are able to slip away peacefully in our arms at home. The advanced state of medicine today is something my wife experienced first hand. She was holding her favourite dog in her arms, believing that it had only had one injection and while she was waiting for the second, it passed away. The dog had already died three minutes earlier and she had not even noticed it slipping away into its own little heaven – and our good old Cäsar

had not either. I hope this will give you a little courage for when the day comes for you to make this difficult call. Always remember that you are helping your dog!

Some dog lovers leave their family member at the veterinarian's surgery to receive the final injection because they are unable to cope with the final goodbye. However, I feel strongly that an owner should stay with his or her dog during this time in return for all the loyalty the dog has offered during its lifetime.

This Bull Terrier's ear doubles as a teething-ring.   *Photo: Moschner.*

Chapter Six

BREEDING

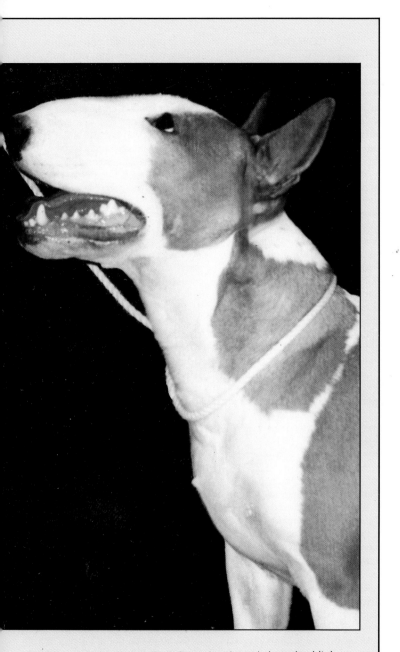

Head study of 'Bullyview Flash Dance', coloured champion bitch, Sandawana Trophy, 1992.

Photo: Dr. Fleig.

GENETICS

Successful breeding relies on taking a long term view and thinking in terms of generations of dogs rather than the short term offspring. Anybody who is seriously contemplating taking up the challenge of breeding dogs should take heed – dog breeding is not a hobby and should never be pursued in order to allow a bitch at least one litter, for the sake of her health or the development of her temperament (which, incidentally, has not been proved to have any marked effect), or just to allow her the experience of motherhood. Only excellent Bull Terriers, whose ancestors as well as their brothers and sisters possess proven first class anatomy and a typical Bull Terrier temperament, should be used for breeding.

The appearance or outer shell, of a dog only displays the phenotype which provides the first notion of what a future litter may look like. This phenotype is determined by the relevant dominant genes. You will find further information on the genotype of a dog, or its genetic shadow, in the pedigree document and, through the thorough reading of this, you will gain a greater insight into pedigree research. The genotype is not only determined by the dominant genes, but by all recessive genes as well. It tends to differ more or less from the phenotype, however, it is the genotype which determines breeding success. I would recommend that anyone who is truly serious about becoming a dog breeder should seek out specialist literature to gain a greater understanding.

This short introduction should have already alerted you to the fact that dog breeding involves a great deal of responsibility and requires substantial knowledge. With such knowledge you can evaluate a breeder, when buying a whelp, by asking him about his motives for a particular mating. One thing is certain – the mating of two world champions does not guarantee a world class litter but, more often than not, results in some very average puppies. For it is the genotype of the parents which determines the outcome and not the phenotype. Good breeders can be recognised by the approach that they take; they focus on a solid construction of a breed line over many generations rather than pleasing themselves with glittering show successes of their stud dogs and bitches. Unfortunately, I have found that it is only every other breeder – perhaps maybe only every fourth breeder – who knows the difference between phenotype and genotype. This is a very sad state of affairs!

PRIORITISING TRAITS

In 1987, I published a comprehensive guide on the techniques of dog breeding. This book demanded a completely new attitude of all breeders and the setting of new priorities – health, intelligence, performance and, finally, beauty! Insiders know, of course, that since the publication of this book some years ago, most breeders have maintained their focus on the criterion 'beauty title', although the relevant national dog breed organisations assume the above order. Well, that is the curse of the large number of famous dog shows and it tends to be they that determine the breeding!

In most cases, at shows, it is impossible to properly evaluate three of the four vital characteristics – health, intelligence and performance.

I am pretty certain that ninety percent of all readers of this guide, and all purchasers of a puppy, agree with my priorities. They want a healthy, intelligent, productive – and beautiful dog. But doesn't anyone reiterate this order of priorities to the breeders? It is you, dear dog lovers, who determine which dogs are used for breeding purposes, whether they be healthy, well-proportioned dogs or of poor temperament and bred exclusively for show purposes.

If you read Chapters Seven and Eight of this guide carefully, you will see that success at dog shows is by no means everything.

Why should you purchase a Bull Terrier if the breeding merely focuses on the creation of beauty which – and I say this mildly – has not exactly promoted the health of these dogs.

When will breeders finally realise that it should be their priority to breed Bull Terriers for dog lovers, creating really affectionate family members which will enrich an owner's life for twelve to fifteen years? In order to enjoy long-term harmonious family life, a dog needs to maintain its fitness and health well into old age and, for full integration into today's society, intelligence and performance are certainly required. Please do not misinterpret the term performance in this instance – I refer to the specific breed performance, as required by the Breed Standard, i.e. a hound must be able to hunt and a shepherd dog must be able to guard. So what of the Bull Terrier? What is this breed's special niche? The Bull Terrier's true performance lies in its best possible adaptation to our human family life.

Although I listed beauty in fourth place on my priority list, it still remains an important breeding objective! The photographs and drawings in this guide clearly demonstrate that the Bull Terrier is a beautiful dog. One should not forget that many requirements stipulated in the Breed Standard refer to anatomical features which are vital for the health of our dogs – solid closely-knit body, strong muscles, good mobility, smooth movements – these all are, and will continue to be, crucial breeding objectives!

I am simply trying to point out that at dog shows, quite naturally, only the outer features of a dog may be properly evaluated while psychological matters remain difficult to assess or may not even be considered. In the case of many breeds, this procedure has awarded many stupid or rather single-sidedly developed kennel dogs champion titles.

Believe me, over many years, I have have watched very carefully, how Bull Terriers with a weak temperament or strong aggressive tendencies have been awarded championship titles for their beautiful appearance, with their negative traits being underplayed by clever handling. I have also witnessed the dreadful impact that such dogs have had on the temperament of their litters – children, grandchildren and great-grandchildren. It is foolish and short-sighted to assume that a champion dog is suitable for breeding purposes without a full analysis of its character and temperament. Breeders should always remember that it is the temperament, the unique breed character, the White Knight, that make dog fanciers purchase a Bull Terrier. Playfulness, a clown-spirit, intelligence, charm, a breed difficult to irritate and one which is open-minded toward humans and other animals – this is what makes our Bull Terriers so wonderful.

The classic White Bull Terrier, this is Judy Alemannentrutz.

Photo: Dr. Fleig

Black/brindle Bull Terrier, this is the 1985 world champion, McWilliams Molly Malone.

Photo: Baptiste, Holland.

Why is it that the breed clubs worldwide do not develop a sensible approach to promote and maintain the unique psychological qualities of our Bull Terrier?

I have often noted discussions in the media over the issue of creating an ideal dog for the year 2000. Perhaps people have not quite realised it yet, but this dog already exists! There is no need at all to create a new breed! No other breed embraces so many positive qualities as the Bull Terrier and, at the same time, requires a suitable owner.

A note for all pedigree breeder's – breed healthy, intelligent, family-orientated – and beautiful Bull Terriers! Never – and I say it again – never comprise the breeding of Bull Terriers which possess a solid temperament, are good-natured and kind. The priority of breeding must be the maintenance and promotion of the unique Bull Terrier temperament.

SPECIFIC BREEDING PROBLEMS

Lack of space does not permit me to give a full and detailed account of the breeding process from mating to the sale of the pups. If you would like to know more about this, may I recommend that you consult a guide which specifically sets out to explain this procedure. Here, in this guide, I will focus on the following key issues which are significant in the breeding of Bull Terriers:

a) Natural mating behaviour
b) Rearing problems
c) Combining Bulldog type and Terrier type

NATURAL MATING BEHAVIOUR

The natural mating behaviour of this breed is not particularly encouraging. Jack Mildenhall, an internationally-renowned Bull Terrier expert, emphasises in his guide '*Bully for me*', that most of the matings of dogs of this breed constitute rapes brought about by humans. Experts simply say that this situation is the result of the historical background of this breed and this harks back to the cruel dog fights which took place in the last century – after all, fights to the death of male dogs against bitches were not unusual. Ethologists speculate that there was a change in the genetic make up of these dogs resulting from the breeding programmes which focused so heavily on fighting success in the pit. This selective breeding is thought to have resulted in a certain amount of gene loss which inhibited the Bull Terrier's ability to display normal social behaviour.

I have been keeping Bull Terriers, both male dogs and bitches, for over 30 years and, over an uninterrupted period of 25 years, we kept some stud dogs. According to my own experience, it is not the gene loss that represents the basic problem but the fact that far too few Bull Terriers are given the opportunity to learn proper social behaviour patterns and have difficulty in successfully relating to other dogs. In order to develop normal dog behaviour patterns, all dog whelps require ample social contact with adolescent and adult dogs which gives them the opportunity to learn respect for one another. In the case of Bull Terriers, the establishment of such contact is, without doubt, made more difficult as they are constantly kept on the lead and there is often a reticence to allow natural contact with other dogs through fear of this resulting in fighting. Irresponsibility on the part of owners who accept the 'locking-up' of these dogs, especially those even consider it to be a breed specific, greatly contributed to the warped development in this area.

Let me say this rather plainly, but hopefully all the easier to understand, we must give our Bull Terriers every opportunity to develop the correct social behaviour toward their own kind. Any resulting aggression should be counteracted by providing appropriate training.

Bull Terriers which grow up in contact with other dogs and are are properly trained, should demonstrate normal behaviour patterns during mating. Always provided that the correct mating date is chosen, a dream wedding may be possible. During the long period of time that I kept stud dogs, no compulsory matings took place. If, during an attempted mating, bride and groom did not unite peacefully, the mating was called off and this is the attitude that should be adopted by all breeders.

So, why are there mating problems? These occur because breeders do nothing to counteract the lacking social behaviour and disproportionate aggressiveness at breeding level. Again, these are features which may not be detected at a dog show and can easily escape the judge's eye. However, the owners of stud dogs and bitches will be well aware of these failings. If such dogs are accepted for breeding, despite these faults, then this has nothing to do with good breeding, but more to do with irresponsibility and the desire to make a decent profit.

REARING PROBLEMS

In the case of the Bull Terrier rearing problems have been documented which may be attributed to an underdeveloped care instinct in the bitch. Jack Mildenhall's book 'Bully for me', includes documented accounts of how some Bull Terrier bitches try to get rid of their litter. It is likely that this type of behaviour has resulted from the fighting dog qualities of the past and a subsequent breeding selection which veers toward the creation of aggression as opposed to sensible social behaviour.

During the time that I was an active breeder, I constantly kept an eye on my Bull Terrier pups, night and day, and therefore, managed to rear all of the litter safely. I have to admit that this close monitoring proved justified in the case of most of my bitches. Registrations at breed clubs reflect the problems of inadequate maternal care in this breed and documentation shows quite clearly how some breeders fail to provide sufficient monitoring, resulting in a high puppy death rate caused by inexperienced or aggressive Bull Terrier bitches. Sadly, it is often the case that where the breeder fails to provide this monitoring, then bitches may kill or crush their young.

Jack Mildenhall and other Bull Terrier experts expressly warn breeders against leaving the litter alone with the mother during the first weeks, but is this a necessary precaution? I think that one has to look at this problem analytically. Quite rightly, ethologists prioritise natural care instincts and good maternal characteristics. Should this really not also apply to the Bull Terrier? May one ignore this quality in a breed?

The fact of the matter is that, today, there are a large number of Bull Terrier bitches which give birth to their pups without any problems, and go on to rear them affectionately and train them properly. I have to admit, however, that many of these bitches are the less beautiful dogs when compared to the Breed Standard and possess physical faults. This problem requires the breeder to make a clear decision. Which is more important – natural breeding behaviour and healthy maternal instincts or beauty? As long as selection in dog breeding is largely based around elements such as missing premolar teeth, faulty colours compared with the requirement of the Breed Standard and, in the case of some Standards, even the presence of dew-claws, why not concentrate on correcting maternal instincts?

For all those of you who intend to become seriously involved in breeding, may I give the following recommendation: Find a bitch from a family which possesses a genotype with good, proper maternal instincts and with breed lines which are dominated by reliable bitches and work on your pups affectionately and with due care. Believe me, bitches which lack the necessary maternal instincts will only continue to constitute a problem for sensible Bull Terrier breeding. Set your priorities in accordance with the ethologists – no doubt, you will have a long and difficult task ahead of you but, should you pursue this, you will be making a lasting contribution in the improvement of this breed's health!

COMBINING BULLDOG TYPE AND TERRIER TYPE

It is exceptionally difficult to produce a uniform appearance in a dog breed which has been created using two very different initial breeds. In the current written Breed Standard document, a harmonious combination of the initial breeds has been achieved. However, the day to day breeding business is dominated by genes and, in the case of the Bull Terrier, these derive from both the Bulldog and the Terrier.

Some twenty to thirty years ago, both initial breed types were more or less noticeable. Today, however, the heavier, slightly short-legged Bulldog type (with visibly weak front, hindquarters and ligaments) is increasingly seen. In the early days, breeding alternatives were available. A number of breeders focussed their breeding efforts on producing the Terrier type and these dogs could be used to make any necessary corrections. Today, for reasons I am unaware of, the elegant, long-legged Terrier type has almost disappeared and this is definitely an ill-conceived move in this breed's development! The 1986 revision of the Standard included the sentence: 'The length of an adult dog's forelegs should approximately correspond to the depth of its chest'. With the situation as it stands today, you have to search very hard to find such a Bull Terrier at a show or, indeed, to find a judge who puts it forward. I can only see the disappearance of the Terrier type over the last few years as a seriously wrong development and one which desperately requires firm breeding action. Under no circumstances, should Bull Terriers be allowed to develop into Bassets!

I have discussed this very issue in depth with Raymond Oppenheimer who clearly agreed with me that the breeding development toward the heavy short-legged Bulldog type requires corrective measures. For him personally, it was impossible to make corrections in his own breed line, but it would promote the health and balance of this breed if breeders and judges would recognise this urgent matter and take the necessary action to redress the balance in this breed in the near future before the Terrier types disappear completely.

PRODUCING COLOURED VARIETIES

'A good dog does not have a bad colour!' I already underlined this perception (which actually derives from horse breeding) in my explanations of the Standard phrases. Where breeding is concerned, the priorities are a good Bull Terrier temperament and anatomy, and colour is a matter of personal taste which is subject to change – a fact we are all well aware of.

In my experience, 'first time buyers' mostly ask for a coloured Bull Terrier whilst the White Knight is the Bull Terrier of experts and fanciers. However, there is no doubt whatsoever, that the wide range of coloured varieties of this breed has contributed quite considerably toward the worldwide popularity that the breed enjoys today.

Among the coloured varieties, the tabby Bull Terrier is certainly the most popular variety with fanciers. One should be aware that a tabby whelp is only produced when at least one of its parents carries the gene for the tabby colouring. These genes may exclusively be found in tabby and black/brindle dogs and all white varieties which possess tabby markings.

White Bull Terriers have to be considered as coloured varieties with regard to the transmission of colours. The white factor suppresses the occurrence of colour except for markings on the head or tiny coloured spots on the body. In the case of purely white Bull Terriers this suppression of colour may only be found out by test matings.

The colour red takes second place among the coloured varieties. This refers to a brilliant red colour. The colour fawn – a slightly pale yellowish red – is less popular.

Bull Terriers with a black/tabby coat with white markings (black/brindle) have a very attractive appearance. From a genetic point of view, these dogs are regarded as tabby Bull Terriers in which the colour black has replaced the tabby coat on large areas of the body. However, it is vital that all transitions to the white markings are marked by the tabby colour. Tri-colour Bull Terriers may, at first sight be of similar appearance however, in their case, the transition from black to white is marked by red or yellow colour. They do not possess the gene for the tabby colour!

In the case of the Bull Terrier, an interesting hereditary rule ensures that the crossing of white with white will always produce white puppies, of course some with markings, even if all four grandparents were coloured. The white factor suppresses the colour.

It is also interesting to note the breeding of coloured varieties which are so-called solid colours – Bull Terriers which are almost 100% coloured possessing hardly any white markings at all. In many cases, only a tiny white blaze suggests that this dog is not of solid colour. These solid colours are transmitted onto all later litters. If you cross a solid brindle Bull Terrier with a white or red Bull Terrier, tabby whelps will be produced.

There are a number of other details with regard to breeding

Tabby Bull Terrier, King von der Sonderburg.

Photo: Markus Grossmann.

Red Bull Terrier, Bullyview Flash Dance.

Photo: Dr. Fleig.

Watersplash's Eye of the Sun – a breeder's pride!

Photo: Cynthia Lord-Ruddy.

Tri-colour Bull Terrier.

Photo: Gericke.

coloured varieties, however, lack of space does not allow me to mention them all.

BREEDER'S RESPONSIBILITY

Dog breeding involves taking on a great deal of responsibility, not only in ensuring that more of these dogs are produced but, if at all possible, that the breed as a whole is improved.

The care and well-being of all ensuing litters is also a matter of great importance and it is entirely your responsibility to ensure that these whelps are placed with well-informed owners in suitable homes.

Even if extra care is taken to select the right buyer for your puppies, you cannot eliminate the possibility that a dog may be subject to maltreatment in the future. I take pleasure in remembering a leading British breeder who declined the sale of his whelps to an overseas buyer, saying that there was always the possibility that such a buyer and family could have an accident and die and, if this were to happen, it would be impossible for him, as a British citizen, to get the puppy back due to the strict quarantine regulations. Such care may seem a little over-zealous, however, it certainly deserves our respect!

Self-bred pups should be like much loved children who go on to receive life-long support from their breeder long after they have left home and embarked on lives of their own. Such an approach would certainly put a stop to mass breeding and ensure that all Bull Terriers are bred with their best interests at heart. It would also go a long way to ending the misery and suffering of dogs who find themselves placed with unsuitable owners.

Chapter Seven

SHOWING

Many shows have categories for young handlers.

WHY SHOW YOUR DOG?

I have always found it difficult to encourage all my puppy buyers to present their dogs at a breed show at least twice. The response I have received from them has usually been along the lines of: 'I do not intend to use my dog for breeding purposes', or 'Shows cause the dog unnecessary stress and, to be perfectly honest with you, I have better things to do with my weekends – something which is a lot more fun for both me and my dog!'

Some very attentive readers may have noted that I am referring with some emphasis to a 'breed show', and this is exactly the reason why I am a supporter of dog shows. From a professional point of view, a show should fulfil all the relevant conditions in that adequate space is provided. The dogs should be presented to an experienced, objective judge either in spacious, clearly-arranged rings, in a well-ventilated hall or, indeed, within the grounds of a dedicated open area – such conditions definitely make a visit worthwhile. The judge carefully examines the dog, comparing it to the Breed Standard. The owners or handlers of the dogs placed in first and second position receive an easy to understand written report – in a way a MOT check of their four-legged friends which clearly states whether the dogs are suitable for breeding purposes. In some countries, all participating dogs receive this analysis.

It is vital for responsible breeders to take the opportunity to present their litters. The breed show represents a test stand which reveals whether the breeder has achieved an improvement of a breed through the breeding methods he or she applied or at least was able to maintain the desired Standard.

In previous chapters, I have already mentioned that show success and show failure are the criteria which breeders will look for. Without breed shows, breeding in line with the Standard would be impossible.

Well, I admit that my enthusiasm for dog shows lacks the support of those who only see these events in a short-sighted way. Of course, I am aware that these exhibitions often encourage prestige indulgence for show fanatics. Also, there are incidences where the sportsman-like conduct and fairness described in the relevant publications fail to win through. But why should we let these human weakness deprive us of our participation in what is otherwise an enjoyable event? Look at such behaviour with a sense of humour. Have a look around you – cast your eye over the show area, the boxes and the ring edge. Nowhere else will you find so many people gathered together who are united by their interest and true adoration of the Bull Terrier. And through this common interest, you will have the pleasure of making many new friends which, in some cases, can last a lifetime. At such shows you will not only come across interesting dogs but also enthusiastic supporters who truly have the best interests of their dogs at heart.

Don't let the stress that is generally associated with shows deter you from participating. It is a good experience to show support for the dog show and present your four-legged family member at least once during its lifetime. To succeed in presenting all the pups of the previous year at breed shows would surely be a great step forward. Dedicated breeders would get a clearer picture of what they have achieved in their field and the less fortunate would be given few excuses for their failure.

RING PRESENTATION

So how do you go about presenting your dog properly at a show? As the photograph at the beginning of this chapter shows, nothing could be easier – even a child can do it, and many do! You should find that many shows offer competitive categories for junior participants. I can clearly remember how proud my daughter was when she successfully competed in an English show with a bitch that, at the time, was a total stranger to her.

It might be a good idea to visit a show first without your dog and to take time to study the procedure. Afterwards, you can begin to train your dog at home.

When presenting your dog at a show, always put your Bull Terrier on an elegant show lead. This is usually a thin but quite strong nylon lead which may be extended or reduced in length as required. However, the most important aspect of showing is that the training must be fun for your dog. To begin with, only train your dog for short periods and introduce aspects of training into the regular games that you play with your dog.

Most Bull Terriers love to play ball and so you can use this as a device to aid training. During such games, encourage your dog not to sit down but to stand well-balanced on all four feet with its attentive eyes fixed on the ball. Take the lead in your left hand and the ball in your right and praise and encourage your dog with words such as 'stand!' If the dog is standing awkwardly, walk it for a few steps, then assume the show position again, using the ball to hold its attention. A favourite treat for the dog in the handler's hand

will work perfectly well as an alternative as almost all our four-legged friends enjoy a tasty treat. A piece of cheese, fried liver or a little dry fish – something that makes your dog's mouth water, will encourage its attentiveness with utmost certainty. Assume the correct position and present your dog. To begin with, you should give the treat for excellent presentation work after half a minute and then this time can be gradually increased.

Do not try too hard or for too long. Start with two-minute long sessions and then you can graduate up to five minute bouts. Your dog should think of this presentation work as a fun game to play and will no doubt enjoy it very much. With plenty of praise and some small treats, almost all Bull Terriers will learn the necessary presentation skills needed for a show and will be happy to do so.

The judge will examine the jaw position of a dog and, therefore, your Bull Terrier must be able to remain calm while its teeth are examined. If you train your dog from a young age to lift its flews and have its mouth examined then you should not experience any problems later. Again, this should not be approached as a compulsory exercise. The adult dog is also capable of learning how to show its teeth if you invest enough time and patience and use a suitably gentle approach. To do this, lift the flews and praise your dog lavishly. Try a phrase such as: 'Look what fine teeth we have got here!' and cuddle your dog to show your appreciation. If your dog successfully completes this task, ask a friend to be the judge of your work. Your Bull Terrier should present its teeth happily and with pride, of course, and your friend should show his admiration for such an obedient dog. Do not open the jaws! A good judge is capable of making a judgment by what he sees when the flews are lifted. Only in very few cases or in the examination of the last molar teeth or a small lower jaw are the jaws opened.

Our dogs are by no means statues and so it is vital to see your dog in action to make a good evaluation. This is why an experienced judge will generally ask that the dog be led in a circle in the ring at the beginning of an evaluation. After that he will ask for the dog to trot in a straight line away from him and, then after, that it is led towards him. Some judges prefer to see other running patterns such as triangles. The important thing for the handler is that the Bull Terrier follows him or her happily, with the lead slack and the dog firmly by his or her side in the 'heel' position. This is another new game for your dog to explore during your training sessions at home. The sudden slowing down of the pace, stopping, prancing and lead-biting are not to be encouraged. Your dog should be able to walk alongside you at a swift place yet not too fast.

Don't forget to give plenty of praise during training sessions as this will encourage your dog and assure it that it is carrying out the required task correctly. However, do not encourage too much excitement as you may well end up with the aforementioned prancing and lead-biting behaviour which is not a desirable sight at all at a show.

It is very important that your dog should not be distracted by other competing dogs during the presentation – the presentation game must take priority! Keep your dog calm while its competitors are having their individual examinations. Of course, it may

glance at its neighbours, but, barking and 'being Mister Wild Guy' is out of the question.

Visit several shows and study the correct ring presentations of insiders and train your dog at home accordingly. You will soon find that correct presentation in the ring can be fun for both you and your dog.

MARKS AND TITLES

At dog shows in Britain, there are only four top places in the individual competition – and with twenty or thirty dogs competing for these, there will no doubt be many disappointed handlers. In mainland Europe, dogs are presented in individual categories according to their age. The mark awarded is important and the example of show marks and requirements below are those that must be met in order to achieve the same standards in accordance with European guidelines. A show's organiser will supply guidelines for the Standard along with rules and regulations.

Excellent – The dog closely conforms to the ideal Standard and small imperfections may be tolerated due to its superior characteristics. The dog possesses the typical features of its sex and is in excellent health. It has a balanced character and good temperament and has excellent posture.

Very good – The dog possesses the typical characteristics of its breed with some non-morphological faults which may be tolerated. It is well-proportioned and enjoys good health.

Good – The dog possesses the main characteristics of its breed and, although it has some faults, there is no attempt to conceal these. It enjoys good health.

Sufficient – The dog conforms to

This Bull Terrier, Ch. Abraxas Count on Me, shows perfect presentation on a slack show lead.

Jasmin von der Sonderburg is a multiple show champion.

A show presentation.
Aricon One in the Eye – one of the rare first class Bull Terriers.

The summer shows are particularly enjoyable – the breed club show of the
Austrian Bull Terrier Club, 1983.

the breed type to a passable degree, however it does not possess all the characteristics generally associated with this breed. Its physical condition leaves much to be desired.

I have to say that, although these evaluation guidelines are quite clear, in my personal experience, the majority of judges tend to use some discretion and there may be some discrepancy over the marks awarded. This is why many exhibitors get the impression that a dog which has been awarded the mark 'Very good' is, contrary to the literal meaning of this mark, actually a bad dog. Judges who try to please everybody have led to a large number of misconceptions. My respect goes those judges who exploit the full scale of marks from 'excellent' to 'sufficient' in an honest and objective manner.

There are quite a few much-sought-after championship titles including: World Champion, European Champion, International Champion and Club Champion, and competition for these is tough as successful dogs carry a great deal of prestige and can command high mating fees. Have another look at the chapter on breeding and note the difference between phenotype and genotype as this will help you evaluate champion titles more objectively.

Another important thing to bear in mind is that achieving a championship title due to lack of competition does not make an average dog in any way whatsoever superior. Also, you should not forget that, at many shows, there are a lot of competitors of equal quality. The final judgment often depends on the dog's form on that particular day and certain acceptable preferences of individual judges and, sometimes, simply luck.

Again, achieving a title at a show does not change the quality of your dog at all – your dog will always be your champion! Nevertheless you shouldn't hesitate to congratulate the winner on his or her success and, should you disagree with the judge's final decision, don't loose your head! There will always be other shows – simply try again.

An adorable Bull Terrier puppy at just 10 days old.   *Photo: Dr. Fleig.*

Chapter Eight

HEALTH CARE

Plenty of outdoor exercise is one of the most important elements of natural health care.

KEEPING YOUR DOG IN GOOD HEALTH

Feeding your dog a proper balanced diet, giving it plenty of exercise and keeping it in good conditions in a loving home are the key factors to ensuring that your Bull Terrier leads a long and happy life.

Where diet and exercise are concerned, don't forget that providing too much can be as harmful as providing too little, although it is far easier to over feed your dog than to over-exercise it! Small meals with just a sensible amount of treats should keep your dog in trim.

It is not only its physical health that should concern you – with such an affectionate animal, you need to consider its psychological welfare as well. Your pet should think of your home as a safe haven and it should feel as though it is a vital part of the family.

Monitoring your dog's wellbeing
It is very important to be totally familiar with your dog's normal behaviour patterns as any changes here may indicate the onset of illness or disease. Thanks to your vigilance, the early diagnosis of an illness and its subsequent treatment give your dog the best chance of a full recovery.

However – a word of warning! Bull Terriers have quite a stoic nature and it often takes quite drastic discomfort for them to show distress. Therefore, it is vital that you monitor the health of your dog carefully and follow up any suspicious signs with an examination.

Bull Terriers are the veterinarian's 'dream patient' – not because they develop a lot of illnesses, but because they are so patient during examinations and treatment. A veterinarian assistant once told me: 'Every time a Bull Terrier enters our practice, the sun begins to shine!' However, an essential condition in creating a good patient is, of course, proper training and a tolerance toward other animals which will enable it to exhibit 'good manners' in the waiting room. Only in a very few cases will Bull Terriers display a fear of treatment and, if this is the case, a little extra attention and a friendly chat will almost always do the trick.

VACCINATIONS

Early vaccination of all puppies against the feared 'killer diseases' such as distemper, hepatitis, leptospirosis and parvovirosis is essential and these should always be followed up by boosters where appropriate. Those who have witnessed the terrible effects of these diseases, and have watched many young dogs die or suffer permanent damage, will certainly approve of my recommendation. Proper vaccination of your dog is not a subject to take lightly!

Outside the United Kingdom, it is important to protect your dog against rabies. The first injection is administered at the age of three months and this is followed by annual booster shots. This offers both the animal and human communities vital protection. If your dog comes into contact with this disease through an infected animal, be it domestic or wild, and has had the necessary vaccination, then the old law which states that your dog must be put to sleep no longer applies.

Simply ask your veterinarian to establish a detailed vaccination schedule when you take your dog for its first check-up and you can rest assured that both your pet and family are protected against these killer diseases.

TREATING PARASITE INFESTATIONS

Almost all puppies suffer from intestinal worms (ascarides). By the time of its sale, the puppy should have been wormed and you should demand confirmation of this from the breeder. After this initial treatment, I recommend that you worm your new family member every other month until it is six months old. Your vet or pet supply retailer will be able to recommend a suitable product and you should follow the manufacturer's instructions carefully. Any further worming should be carried out when an infestation is suspected or every six months as a preventative measure. As a safeguard, you may wish to have your dog's motions examined at regular intervals to ensure maximum protection.

Tape worms
Tape worms are fairly common

A little more exercise would certainly help keep the figure in trim. However, at eight years old, one also needs a comfortable bed now and then! *Photo: René Jung.*

and this is a reflection of the higher incidence of flea infestations as fleas are the intermediate hosts for the tape worm. Loss of weight, weakness and tiredness are all signs of an infestation of tape worm. In many cases you may detect individual gourd seed-like worm limbs in your dog's motion. If you suspect the presence of tape worms, take a motion to your veterinarian for examination. He or she will be able to prescribe a medicine that best tackles the particular worm type encountered.

Fleas and lice

Flea infestations have increased and must be treated with a proprietory flea shampoo, followed by flea powder. Fleas do not exclusively live on your dog but will affect the whole of its sleeping area and so its bedding and the surrounding carpet must be treated as well. Be sure to use a product which kills both the adult fleas and their eggs to ensure a thorough and complete treatment of the problem. As with all products of this nature, follow the manufacturer's instructions!

Similar treatments are available to combat lice. However, lice will not infest your dog's sleeping basket or box and its surroundings but live exclusively on your dog.

Mites

Mites cause considerable itching. An infestation of Autumn mites is detectable by the appearance of tiny, orange spots. These mites are easily picked up by your dog in wheat fields and can be eradicated by a medicated bath. Sarcoptic mange is a disease, caused by mites which can also be contagious for humans. Demodectic mange is caused by the demodectic mite and, although these mites may be

found on just about every dog, only dogs with a weak immune system will develop mange. Both forms of mange require immediate veterinary treatment. A hereditary weakness of the immune system has been noted which causes affected dogs to be sensitive to the demodectic mite. Dogs suffering from such a weakness should be excluded from breeding. Some irresponsible breeders have preferred to ignore the consequences of poor breeding lines and, in the case of the Bull Terrier, have created some pedigrees which are affected by this weakness of the immune system.

Ticks

Ticks lurking in forests and fields waiting 'for a bite' represent a real plague for our dogs and you might like to fit your dog with one of the tick protection collars available. Should you detect a tick that has already penetrated your dog's skin, the simplest method of removal is to moisten your fingers with a little spittle and turn the tick's body in swift, light circular movements in an anti-clcockwise direction. If you are successful in getting the tick out, drop it on the ground and crush it with your shoe or burn it. In areas where ticks occur it is recommended that you examine your dog thoroughly after each walk and remove any loose ticks, crushing them between your finger and nails or on the ground with your shoe.

SKIN DISEASES

Today, general pollution of the environment has contributed to the widespread occurrence of skin diseases, affecting both humans and dogs. The Bull Terrier, in particular, has sensitive skin and is more likely to develop a skin disease than many other breeds. This predisposition may be attributed to its white coat and you will see a similar tendency among humans with fair or red hair and pale skin.

Itching – Pruritus is the most commonly encountered of these diseases and may be caused by:
a) an allergic reaction
b) a viral skin irritation
c) psychological factors

In the case of the Bull Terrier, eczema between the toes is encountered quite frequently.

According to my experience and observations, I have noticed a higher occurrence of skin diseases in the white Bull Terrier, however, I am not in a position to confirm that the coloured varieties are not affected to a similar degree.

I do not recommend that you attempt to treat this type of ailment yourself as there are a number of factors which may cause such diseases. Therefore diagnosis and treatment must be dealt with on an individual basis. Should your dog develop problems of this kind, you should consult a veterinarian who has considerable experience concerning the treatment of dermatological diseases. Such special knowledge can spare your dog long periods of suffering caused by ineffective treatment. Veterinarians who have little understanding of dermatology and who would rather 'kill off' a skin disease with Cortisone injections rather than refer your dog to a specialist make my hackles rise.

LAMENESS

Well-muscled breeds such as the Bull Terrier have a certain predisposition for incurring sprains, bruises, dislocations and torn ligaments and a parallel can be drawn with the risk of injury that high performance athletes face. Therefore, it is vital to avoid putting your dog's body under too much strain. Please refer to Chapter Four for further details.

Treating minor injuries
If sprains or dislocations do occur, the application of a splint to the affected area along with plenty of patience will do more good than the injections so eagerly administered by many vets. Encourage your injured dog to take things easy and make sure that it is not romping around, playing with friends or jumping over tables and chairs for at least a couple of weeks. Keep your dog on the lead when you take it for a walk and monitor its behaviour carefully at home and, with sufficient rest, the injury should heal completely. A proper recovery takes time so do not be tempted to rush things as this may result in a permanent weakness which will be susceptible to repeat injuries.

Serious conditions
There are some serious conditions which can cause lameness and, primarily, I would like to mention Patella Luxation. This is a disease of the knee joint which Bull Terriers have a hereditary disposition toward and the condition causes a short-lived, but frequently occurring, dislocation of the patella toward the inner side of the leg. In an affected dog, the joint head at the neck of the thigh bone is steeply positioned and this alters the axis of the extensor muscles of the thigh, resulting in the aforementioned dislocations. In turn these dislocations can cause acute inflammation of the knee joint. This condition can be successfully treated by an operation, however, I would like to

Animal friendship.

Photo: Peter Laschenko.

reiterate that Patella Luxation is a hereditary disease and affected dogs should be excluded from breeding. Unfortunately, this problem has often been totally ignored in the case of the Bull Terrier! Instead, associated breed clubs have preferred to concentrate on the treatment of Hip Joint Dysplasia. In a German study, approximately 750 Bull Terriers were anaesthetised and X-rayed for signs of hip displacement. This expensive procedure may have seemed justifiable at the time but we now know that the occurrence of hip dysplasia is no more significant in Bull Terriers than in other breeds. The results concluded that less than 3% of the Bull Terriers examined showed medium or heavy HD and this suggests that this breed is one of the healthiest with regard to hip problems. Therefore, there are no

genetic reasons to continue with serial HD examinations.

KIDNEY DISEASES

The Bull Terrier breed is, however, affected by hereditary kidney diseases. There are a number of breed lines affected in this way which were produced by breeders who, either negligently or intentionally, ignored the occurrence of renal disorders in order to achieve short-lived show success. Successful diagnosis and treatment of such ailments can be problematic as there may be no discernable external symptoms during the early stages of the disease and detection in many cases often occurs too late. There are new screening methods available which cost only a fraction of the aforementioned HD tests and which allow early detection of hereditary kidney diseases such as Nephritis. It is highly recommended that all Bull Terriers are examined for such diseases prior to their use for breeding purposes, and affected dogs should be excluded. However, so long as breed clubs continue to ignore this recommendation, puppy purchasers are advised to make enquiries as to whether both parents – stud dog and bitch – were examined for kidney disorders.

Even in the case of a pure fancier's dog, where there is no intention of using the dog for breeding, the owner should be extra vigilant for any suspicious signs which may indicate a kidney disorder. It is highly advisable to have a sample of your dog's urine tested if your dog displays any tell-tale signs such as an unusually high level of thirst. Early detection of kidney disease enables quite effective treatment which will prolong your dog's life.

DEAFNESS

In the early years of systematic breeding of the white Bull Terrier,

Bliss is a soft cushion to sleep on.   *Illustration: Michael Walker.*

My best friends!

deafness was considered a serious hereditary disease. In this context I would like to expressly mention that white Bull Terriers are by no means albinos. However, pure white breeds are often genetically affected by deafness; just think of Dalmatians.

The problem of deafness has almost been resolved in the case of the Bull Terrier by establishing coloured varieties and the continued crossing of coloured breed lines with white breed lines. Today the percentage of Bull Terriers affected by deafness lies well below 1% and the Bull Terrier serves as an excellent example of how correct breeding selections can help solve the problems of hereditary disease. However, I have to admit that the motives for the crossing of the coloured varieties with the pure white varieties were primarily based on totally different criteria such as the improvement of bone structure, more bodily substance and a more beautiful head form. Still, breeders who took a long-term view recognised, quite early on, that this crossing with the coloured varieties represented an effective solution for the problem of deafness.

GENERAL HEALTH

Many readers who have taken on board the information in this chapter so far, may be now asking themselves whether they should indeed purchase a Bull Terrier – after all, there are so many diseases associated with this breed. Would it not be better to choose a different breed?

My response to this question is very clear! Almost all dog breeds are associated with a considerable number of predispositions to certain diseases that are typical for that particular breed. I do not feel any obligation to mention them all. Many authors of dog guides feel that it is probably in

the best interest of their breed, its breeders and clubs not to mention such diseases. There are some quite adventurous examples of 'brushing unpleasantries under the carpet'!

I personally do not favour this method of dealing with the tricky issue of disease. At least if you come to the breed with all the information before you, you will be sufficiently well-informed and prepared to cope with all eventualities – this is a more responsible approach to your pet's health than simply going in with your eyes closed and hoping that all will be well. Perhaps you remember my list of breeding priorities – health appears right at the top of the list! I expect open-mindedness from breeders of all breeds and a willingness to co-operate when it comes to the health of our dogs.

Let's return to the Bull Terrier. An average life expectancy of ten years is a good result – however, it could be better. The skin and kidneys are still two very vulnerable areas which can considerably shorten the life span of these dogs and this calls for decisive action on behalf of the breeders!

However, despite the indisputable health problems, few breeds offer so much pleasure.

Appendix

UK BREED CLUBS

The Bull Terrier Club
Mrs M R Weeks, 14 Ashcourt Drive,
Hornsea, East Yorkshire HU18 1EN

Regional Bull Terrier Clubs

Bull Terrier Club of Wales
Mrs M Hughes, Graymor, Greenway
Avenue, Rumney, Cardiff CF3 8HQ

Coloured Bull Terrier Club
Miss P McCombie, Moatville Cottage,
Main Street, Fladbury, Pershore,
Worcestershire WR10 2QB

East Anglian Bull Terrier Club
Miss E Philip, 10 Edgeborough Close,
Kentford, Newmarket, Suffolk CB8 8QY

North East Bull Terrier Club
Mrs S McAllister, 29 Garth 22,
Killingworth, North Tyneside
NE12 0HZ

Northern Provincial Bull Terrier Club
Mr R R Hurst, Richmond, 43 Manor
Drive, Great Boughton, Chester CH3 5QN

Notts & Derby District Bull Terrier Club
Mrs A E Hill, Manor Cottage, Ratcliffe
on Soar, Nottingham NG11

Scottish Bull Terrier Club
Mrs L Shearer, 21 Elliot Crescent,
Calderwood, East Kilbride G74 3ET

South Eastern Counties Bull Terrier
Club
Mrs L McGregor, 70 Raglan Gardens,
Oxhey, Watford, Herts WD1 4LL

Ulster Bull Terrier Club
Mr S Boyle, 14 Lisnahull Park,
Dungannon, Co Tyrone,
Northern Ireland BT70 1UH

West of England Bull Terrier Club
Mr P Rolfe, 1 The Tanyards,
Chandler's Ford, Hampshire
SO5 1TJ

Yorkshire Bull Terrier Club
Mrs E Micklethwaite, 3 Unsliven Road,
Stocksbridge, Sheffield S30 5FT

Miniature Bull Terrier Club
Mrs E Thornley, Clarkson Green Farm,
School Lane, Catforth, Preston,
Lancashire PR4 0HL

US BREED CLUBS

Bull Terrier Club of America
Mrs Susan C Murphy, 10477 Ethel Cr.,
Cypress, CA 90630

Local Clubs

Barbary Coast Bull Terrier Club
Nan Stodder, 612, Haight Avenue,
Alameda, CA92027

Golden State Bull Terrier Club
Lana Chappell, 19600 Mayall Street,
Northridge, CA 91324

Bull Terrier Club of Hawaii
Myra N Tamanaha, P.O. Box 13101,
Kailua, HI 96734

Fort Dearborn Bull Terrier Club
Anita Bartell, 2214 Ash Lane,
Northbrook, IL 60062

Bull Terrier Group of Metropolitan
Detroit
Cleo Parker, 17710 Floral, Livonia,
MI 48152

Bull Terrier Club of St. Louis,
Steve Fletchall, 4398 Hwy HH,
Catawissa, MO 63015

Garden State Bull Terrier Club
Emily Russ, RD 6, Box 230, Blairstown,
NJ 07825

Knickerbocker Bull Terrier Club
Virginia Duce, 340 Dayton Ave.,
Manorville, NY 11949

Bull Terrier Club of Philadelphia
Rhona A. Hausken, 3317 Pierson Dr.,
Wilmington, DE 18910

Golden Triangle Bull Terrier Club
Joyce L. Brown, 120 Summit St.,
West Newton, PA 15089

Bull Terrier Club of Dallas
Kay Davis, Rt3, Box 531, Decatur,
TX 76234

Bull Terrier Club of Puget Sound
Doris Jasp, 7910 128th Street East,
Puyallup, WA 98373

Glossary of dog terminology

Almond eye: The eye set in an almond-shaped surround

Angulation: Angle formed by the bones, mainly the shoulder, forearm, stifle and hock.

Anorchid: Male animal without testicles.

Anus: Anterior opening under the tail.

Backline: Topline of dog from neck to tail.

Bite: The position of the teeth when the mouth is shut.

Bitch: Female dog.

Breastbone: Bone running down the middle of the chest, to which all but the floating ribs are attached; sternum.

Breeder: Someone who breeds dogs.

Brisket: The forepart of the body below the chest between the forelegs.

Brood bitch: Female used for breeding.

Bull neck: A heavy neck, well-muscled.

Canine: Animal of the genus canis which includes dogs, foxes, wolves and jackals.

Canines: The four large teeth in the front of the mouth, two upper and two lower next to incisors.

Carpals: Bones of the pastern joints.

Castrate: To surgically remove the testes of a male.

Cow-hocked: Hocks turned inwards.

Croup: The rear part of the back above the hind legs.

Crown: The highest part of the head: the top of the skull.

Cryptorchid: A male dog with neither testicle descended.

Cull: To eliminate unwanted puppies.

Dam: Mother of the puppies.

Dew claw: Extra claw on the inside lower portion of legs.

Down-faced: Tip of nose below level of stop.

Elbow: The joint between the upper arm and forearm.

Expression: The general appearance of all features of the head as typical of the breed.

Femur: The large heavy bone of the thigh between the pelvis and stifle joint.

Flank: Side of the body between the last rib and the hip.

Flews: The inside of the lips.

Forearm: Front leg between elbow and pastern.

Foreface: Front part of the head before the eyes; the muzzle.

Gait: A style of movement.

Handler: A person who handles (shows) a dog at dog shows, field trials or obedience tests.

Hare foot: A long narrow foot.

Haw: A third eyelid at the inside corner of the eye.

Heat: An alternative word for 'season' in bitches.

Heel: Command by handler to keep the dog close to his heel.

Heel free: Command whereby the dog must walk to heel without a lead.

Height: Vertical measurements from withers to ground.

Hip dysplasia: Malformation of the ball of the hip joint.

Hock: Lower joint of the hind-legs.

Hucklebones: Top of the hip bones.

Humerus: Bone of the upper arm.

In-breeding: The mating of closely related dogs of the same standard.

Incisors: Upper and lower front teeth between the canines.

Ischium: Hipbone.

In season: On heat, ready for mating.

Inter-breeding: The breeding together of different varieties.

Jowls: Flesh of lips and jaws.

Level bite: The upper and lower teeth edge to edge.

Line breeding: The mating of related dogs within a line or family to a common ancestor, ie dog to grand-dam or bitch to grand-sire.

Litter: The pups from one whelping.

Loin: Either side of the vertebrae column between the last rib and hip bone.

Mate: The sex act between the dog and bitch.

Milk teeth: First teeth. (Puppies lose these at four to six months.)

Molars: Rear teeth.

Monorchid: A male animal with only one testicle in the scrotum.

Muzzle: The head in front of the eyes, including nose, nostril and jaws.

Nose: The ability to scent.

Occiput: The rear of the skull.

Oestrum: The period during which a bitch has her menstrual flow and can be mated.

Out-crossing: The mating of unrelated individuals of the same breed.

Overshot: Front teeth (incisors) of the upper jaw overlap and do not touch the teeth of the lower jaw.

Pads: The tough, cushioned soles of the feet.

Paper foot: A flat foot with thin pads.

Pastern: Foreleg between the carpus and the digits.

Patella: Knee cap composed of cartilage at the stifle joint.

Pedigree: The written record of the names of a dog's ancestors.

Pelvis: Set of bones attached to the end of the spinal column.

Pigeon-toed: With toes pointing in.

Puppy: A dog up to 12 months of age.

Quarters: The two hindlegs.

Scapula: The shoulder blade.

Scissor bite: The outside of the lower incisors touches the inner side of the upper incisors.

Second thigh: The part of the hindquarters from stifle to hock.

Set on: Insertion or attachment of tail or ears.

Set up: Posed so as to make the most of the dog's appearance for the show ring.

Sire: A dog's male parent.

Spay: To surgically remove the ovaries to prevent conception.

Splay feet: Feet with toes spread wide.

Spring of ribs: Curvature of ribs for heart and lung capacity.

Stance: Manner of standing.

Standard: The standard of perfection for a breed.

Sternum: The brisket or breast bone.

Stifle: The hindlegs above the hock.

Stop: Indentation between the eyes.

Stud: Male used for breeding.

Tail set: How the base of the tail sets on the rump.

Thigh: Hindquarters from hip to stifle.

Topline: The dog's outline from just behind the withers to the tail set.

Type: The characteristic qualities distinguishing a breed; the embodiment of the standards essentials.

Undershot: The front teeth of the lower jaw projecting or overlapping the front teeth of the upper jaw.

Upper arm: The humerus or bone of the foreleg between shoulder blade and the forearm.

Vent: The anal opening.

Whelp: The act of giving birth.

Withers: The highest point of the shoulders just behind the neck.

Wry mouth: Mouth in which the lower jaw does not line up with the upper.